SEARCH ENGINE OPTIMIZATION

Author's

Ms. V.Priyanka

Dr. J.Jayashree

Mr. R.Yuvaraj

Mr. Jinto Sebastian

Mr. Ganesh Babu.B

SHANLAX
#SINCE1990
SHANLAX PUBLICATIONS

Title:	**Search Engine Optimization**
Author's Name:	**Ms. V.Priyanka** **Dr. J.Jayashree** **Mr. R.Yuvaraj** **Mr. Jinto Sebastian** **Mr. Ganesh Babu.B**
Published by:	**Shanlax Publications,** **Vasantha Nagar, Madurai – 625003,** **Tamil Nadu, India**
Publisher's Address:	**61, 66 T.P.K. Main Road,** **Vasantha Nagar, Madurai – 625003,** **Tamil Nadu, India**
Printer's Details:	**Shanlax Press, 66 T.P.K. Main Road,** **Vasantha Nagar, Madurai – 625003,** **Tamil Nadu, India**
Edition Details (I,II,III):	**I**
ISBN:	**978-81-19337-39-2**
Month & Year:	**November, 2023**

Pages:	**181**
Price:	**₹ 270/-**

PREFACE

Search Engine Optimization (SEO) and Search Engine Management (SEM) is the art and the science of getting website to appear prominently in organic search engine result when a search submits a query relevant to that website.

Welcome to the dynamic world of Search Engine Management (SEM), a field that lies at the intersection of technology, marketing, and user experience. As we navigate through the vast landscape of the digital realm, the ability to harness the power of search engines has become a critical component for businesses and individuals alike.

This preface serves as an introduction to the exciting journey you are about to embark on - a journey that will unravel the complexities of search engine algorithms, keywords, and online advertising. Whether you are a seasoned marketing professional looking to enhance your skills or a newcomer eager to understand the intricacies of SEM, this guide is designed to provide you with the knowledge and tools necessary to navigate this ever-evolving landscape.

Search Engine Management, often used interchangeably with Search Engine Marketing, encompasses a range of strategies aimed at improving a website's visibility on search engine results pages. With search engines acting as the digital gatekeepers to information, products, and services, mastering SEM is essential for businesses seeking to thrive in the competitive online marketplace.

In the chapters that follow, we will delve into the core principles of SEM, from the fundamentals of search engine optimization (SEO) to the intricacies of pay-per-click (PPC) advertising. We will explore the latest trends, industry best practices, and innovative techniques that will empower you to create effective SEM campaigns and drive meaningful results.

The digital landscape is ever-changing, and staying ahead requires a continuous commitment to learning and adapting. This guide is designed to be a valuable resource, providing insights, strategies, and practical tips to help you not only understand the principles of SEM but also apply them strategically to achieve your goals.

As we embark on this SEM journey together, I encourage you to approach each chapter with curiosity and enthusiasm. The world of search engines is a fascinating and dynamic one, filled with opportunities for those who are willing to explore, learn, and implement the strategies outlined in the pages ahead.

Get ready to unlock the potential of Search Engine Management and elevate your online presence to new heights.

INDEX

CHAPTER - I

1.1 Definition of SEM:

Search Engine Management (SEM) is a digital marketing strategy and online advertising technique focused on increasing the visibility and prominence of a website or web page in search engine results pages (SERPs). SEM primarily involves the use of paid advertising, often referred to as pay-per-click (PPC) advertising, to ensure that a website or specific web content is displayed prominently in search engine results for relevant keywords or search queries. SEM can also encompass various other activities aimed at optimizing a website's performance in search engines, such as search engine optimization (SEO).

Key components of Search Engine Management:

1. **Pay-Per-Click (PPC) Advertising**: This is the most common form of SEM, where advertisers bid on specific keywords or search terms, and their ads are displayed prominently in search results when those keywords are used in a search query. Advertisers pay a fee each time a user clicks on their ad, hence the name "pay-per-click."
2. **Keyword Research:** SEM campaigns begin with in-depth keyword research to identify the most relevant and high-performing keywords that potential customers use when searching for products, services, or information related to a business.
3. **Ad Creation**: Creating compelling and relevant ads is essential for SEM success. These ads typically include a

headline, description, and a link to the landing page. The goal is to entice users to click on the ad and visit the advertiser's website.

4. **Landing Page Optimization**: To maximize the effectiveness of SEM campaigns, the landing page (the page users land on after clicking the ad) should be optimized for both user experience and conversion. This includes ensuring fast loading times, clear call-to-actions, and relevant content.
5. **Bid Management**: Advertisers adjust their bids for specific keywords based on factors like budget constraints and competition to ensure their ads remain competitive in the ad auction.
6. **Ad Placement**: SEM allows advertisers to specify where and when their ads are displayed, including geographical targeting and scheduling ads to appear during specific times or days.
7. **Performance Monitoring and Analysis**: Continuous monitoring and analysis of SEM campaigns are crucial to assess their effectiveness. Advertisers use analytics tools to track metrics such as click-through rates (CTR), conversion rates, and return on investment (ROI) to make data-driven decisions for campaign optimization.

SEM is often used as part of a broader online marketing strategy alongside other techniques like search engine optimization (SEO) to improve a website's organic search rankings. Together, these approaches help businesses increase their online visibility, drive more traffic to their websites, and ultimately achieve their marketing and sales goals

1.2 Introduction to SEM:

SEM, which stands for Scanning Electron Microscope, is a powerful and versatile scientific instrument used for imaging and analyzing the microstructure of a wide range of materials. It is a type of electron microscope, a class of instruments that use a focused beam of electrons to magnify and visualize objects at a much higher resolution than traditional optical microscopes. SEMs offer several advantages over other imaging techniques, making them invaluable tools in various fields of science and industry.

Here's an introduction to SEM and its key features:

1. **Principle of Operation:** SEM works based on the interaction between a focused electron beam and the sample. When the electron beam strikes the specimen, it induces various signals, including secondary electrons, backscattered electrons, X-rays, and cathodoluminescence. These signals are detected and used to create images and gather information about the sample's composition and topography.
2. **Resolution:** SEMs provide exceptionally high resolution, typically in the range of nanometers. This allows researchers to visualize fine details on the surface of specimens, making them suitable for studying the microstructure of materials.
3. **Magnification:** SEMs offer a wide range of magnification options, from 10x to over 300,000x, making them suitable for examining a broad spectrum of sample sizes, from macroscopic objects to nano scale structures.

4. **Sample Preparation**: Samples for SEM analysis need to be properly prepared. This often involves coating non-conductive specimens with a thin layer of conductive material (e.g., gold) to prevent charging effects. Samples can be solid, powdered, biological, or even fractured materials.

1. **Imaging Modes:**
   - **Secondary Electron Imaging (SEI):** This mode provides topographical information and is particularly useful for surface analysis.
   - **Backscattered Electron Imaging (BEI):** BEI reveals differences in atomic number (composition) and is used for material contrast imaging.
   - **X-ray Analysis (EDS or EDX):** Energy-dispersive X-ray spectroscopy allows for elemental analysis of the sample.

Cathodoluminescence (CL): CL can be used to study the optical properties of a sample.

1. **Applications:** SEMs find applications in a wide range of scientific and industrial fields, including materials science, geology, biology, nanotechnology, metallurgy, archaeology, and more. They are essential for characterizing the microstructure, morphology, and composition of various materials.
2. **Environmental SEM (ESEM):** Some SEMs are equipped for environmental imaging, allowing the examination of specimens under controlled gas or liquid conditions. This is particularly useful for studying biological samples or hydrated materials.

3. **3D Imaging:** Advanced SEM techniques, such as serial sectioning and electron tomography, enable the reconstruction of three-dimensional images of samples, providing insights into their internal structures.

SEM is a versatile and indispensable tool for researchers and scientists who need to explore the micro-world with high precision and detail. It continues to evolve with advancements in technology, enabling more comprehensive and sophisticated analyses of a wide array of materials and biological specimens.

1.3 Introduction Ad Words:

"Google AdWords," which is now known as "Google Ads." Google Ads is an online advertising platform developed by Google that allows businesses and advertisers to display advertisements on Google's search engine results pages (SERPs), websites, and other online platforms. It's a powerful tool for reaching a wide audience and promoting products or services.

Here's a brief introduction to Google Ads:

1. **Ad Campaign Creation:** With Google Ads, you can create and manage advertising campaigns. These campaigns consist of ad groups, keywords, and ads.
2. **Keyword Targeting:** One of the key features of Google Ads is the ability to target specific keywords. Your ads will appear when users search for these keywords on Google.
3. **Ad Types:** Google Ads supports various ad formats, including text ads, image ads, video ads, and more. You can choose the format that best suits your advertising goals.

4. **Bidding:** You set a budget for your advertising campaign and bid for ad placements. You can choose between cost-per-click (CPC), cost-per-thousand-impressions (CPM), or cost-per-acquisition (CPA) bidding strategies.
5. **Ad Placement:** Your ads can appear on the Google search network (on Google's search results pages) or the Google Display Network (on other websites that partner with Google to display ads).
6. **Ad Targeting:** You can target your ads based on various criteria, such as location, demographics, interests, and more. This allows you to reach a specific audience.
7. **Ad Performance Tracking:** Google Ads provides detailed analytics and reporting to help you track the performance of your ads. You can see data on clicks, impressions, conversions, and more.
8. **Budget Control:** You have full control over your advertising budget. You can set daily or monthly limits to ensure you don't overspend.
9. **Conversion Tracking:** Google Ads allows you to track conversions, such as website purchases, sign-ups, or phone calls, to measure the effectiveness of your campaigns.
10. **Ad Quality:** Google uses a Quality Score system to assess the relevance and quality of your ads. A higher Quality Score can lead to lower costs and better ad placements.
11. **Ad Extensions:** You can enhance your ads with various extensions, such as callout, site link, and location extensions, to provide additional information to potential customers.

Google Ads can be a highly effective way to drive traffic to your website, generate leads, and increase sales. However, it can be complex, and success often requires careful planning, monitoring, and optimization of your campaigns. It's essential to do thorough keyword research, create compelling ad copy, and continually refine your strategy to get the best results from Google Ads.

Google Ad Words:

Google Ads, formerly known as Google AdWords, is an online advertising platform developed by Google. It allows advertisers to display their ads on Google's search engine results pages, partner websites, and other Google properties. Google Ads is one of the most popular and widely used online advertising platforms, enabling businesses to promote their products and services to a vast online audience.

Here are some key components and features of Google Ads:

1. **Keywords:** Advertisers select relevant keywords related to their products or services. When users search for those keywords on Google, the advertiser's ads may appear.
2. **Ad Campaigns:** Advertisers create campaigns to group related ads and keywords. Each campaign can have its own budget, targeting options, and settings.
3. **Ad Groups:** Within each campaign, advertisers create ad groups to further segment their ads and keywords. Ad groups help ensure that ads are highly relevant to the search terms.
4. **Ad Creatives**: Advertisers create text, image, or video ads that are shown to users. These ads typically include a headline, description, and a call-to-action.

5. **Bidding**: Advertisers set bids for their keywords. This is the maximum amount they are willing to pay for a click on their ad. Google uses a bidding system to determine which ads appear in what order.
6. **Ad Extensions:** Advertisers can add extensions to their ads to provide additional information like phone numbers, locations, links to specific pages on their website, and more.
7. **Quality Score**: Google assigns a Quality Score to each keyword, which is based on the relevance of the keyword to the ad and the quality of the landing page. Higher Quality Scores can lead to better ad placement and lower costs.
8. **Targeting Options:** Advertisers can choose various targeting options, including location, language, demographics, devices, and more to reach their desired audience.
9. **Conversion Tracking:** Advertisers can track actions users take on their website after clicking on an ad. This helps measure the effectiveness of their campaigns
10. **Budget Management:** Advertisers can set daily or monthly budgets to control their spending on ads.
11. **Ad Performance Analysis:** Google Ads provides detailed reports and analytics to measure the performance of ads and campaigns, allowing advertisers to make data-driven decisions.

Google Ads is a pay-per-click (PPC) advertising platform, which means advertisers only pay when someone clicks on their ads. The cost per click (CPC) can vary depending on the competition for the chosen keywords and the quality of the ads.

It's important to note that Google Ads is a complex platform, and successful advertising campaigns often require careful planning, continuous optimization, and a good understanding of online advertising principles. Many businesses and advertisers use Google Ads to reach a wider audience and drive traffic to their websites, ultimately leading to increased sales and conversions.

1.4 Account Management:

Account management is a business practice or function that involves building and maintaining relationships with customers, clients, or accounts to ensure their needs and expectations are met. It is a key component of customer relationship management (CRM) and is often used in B2B (business-to-business) or high-value B2C (business-to-consumer) scenarios.

The primary objectives of account management typically include:

1. **Customer Satisfaction:** Ensuring that customers are happy with the products or services they receive and addressing any issues or concerns they may have.
2. **Customer Retention**: Fostering long-term relationships with customers to encourage repeat business and loyalty.
3. **Upselling and Cross-Selling:** Identifying opportunities to sell additional products or services to existing customers.
4. **Account Growth:** Supporting the growth of customer accounts by understanding their evolving needs and offering solutions that align with those needs.
5. **Problem Resolution:** Addressing customer complaints, concerns, or issues in a timely and effective manner.

6. **Communication:** Maintaining open and clear lines of communication between the company and the customer to ensure mutual understanding and alignment.

Account managers, also known as key account managers or client relationship managers, are typically responsible for implementing account management strategies. They work closely with their clients, getting to know their businesses and industries in detail, so they can provide personalized and tailored solutions. In essence, account management is about nurturing and maintaining valuable business relationships to achieve mutual success and benefit both the company and its clients.

Features of Account Management;

Account management typically refers to the processes and activities involved in managing customer or user accounts in various contexts, such as in businesses, organizations, or online platforms. The specific features of account management can vary depending on the context, but here are some common features and functionalities associated with account management:

1. **User Registration:** Allows users to create new accounts by providing necessary information, such as username, password, email, and personal details.
2. **User Authentication:** Verifies the identity of users when they log in, often through methods like username / password, biometrics (fingerprint or facial recognition), or two-factor authentication (2FA).
3. **User Profiles:** Allows users to manage and update their personal information, including contact details, profile pictures, and preferences.

4. **User Permissions:** Defines roles and permissions for different user types, specifying what actions and data each type of user can access or modify.
5. **Password Management:** Enables users to reset or change their passwords, implement password policies (e.g., complexity requirements), and securely store password information.
6. **Access Control:** Controls and tracks user access to resources or data, often using role-based access control (RBAC) or similar mechanisms.
7. **User Activity Logging:** Records and logs user actions and interactions within the system for security, compliance, and audit purposes.
8. **User Deactivation and Deletion:** Allows administrators to deactivate or delete user accounts as needed, including archiving user data.
9. **Account Recovery:** Provides mechanisms for users to regain access to their accounts if they forget their passwords or face other login issues.
10. **Session Management:** Tracks and manages user sessions, including the ability to log users out or terminate sessions to enhance security.
11. **Email Notifications:** Sends automated emails to users for account-related events like registration confirmation, password resets, or account activity alerts.
12. **Account Verification:** May include email or phone number verification to ensure the authenticity of user accounts.
13. **Account Lockout:** Implements security measures to lock out or suspend accounts temporarily after a certain number of failed login attempts.

14. **Data Privacy and Compliance:** Complies with data protection regulations (e.g., GDPR) by providing options for users to control their data and respect their privacy.
15. **Customer Support Integration:** Allows users to seek help, contact support, or resolve account-related issues through the system.

These features help organizations manage and secure user accounts, provide a good user experience, and ensure compliance with legal and regulatory requirements, depending on the specific needs of the business or platform.

1.5 Campaign and Ad Group Management :

Campaign and ad group management are essential components of online advertising, particularly in the context of pay-per-click (PPC) advertising, such as Google Ads or Microsoft Advertising (formerly Bing Ads). These terms refer to the structured organization and control of your advertising efforts to achieve specific marketing objectives.

1. Campaign Management:

Definition: Campaign management involves the planning, execution, and monitoring of a set of advertisements, often with a shared goal, budget, and target audience. A campaign is typically focused on a particular product, service, or marketing objective.

Key Components:

Campaign Goals: Clearly define the objectives you want to achieve, such as generating leads, driving sales, increasing brand awareness, or website traffic.

Budget Allocation: Decide how much you're willing to spend on the entire campaign, and allocate budgets for specific advertising platforms (e.g., Google Ads, Facebook Ads).

Ad Content: Create and optimize ads (text, images, videos) that align with your campaign's goals.

Targeting: Specify the audience you want to reach based on demographics, location, interests, and other factors.

Scheduling: Determine when your ads will run, which can include specific times of day or days of the week.

Example: If you're a shoe retailer, you might create a "Summer Shoe Sale" campaign to promote discounted summer footwear. This campaign will have its budget, ad creatives, and targeting settings.

2.Ad Group Management:

Definition: Ad group management is the process of organizing and optimizing a set of related ads within a campaign. Ad groups are smaller segments within a campaign that target specific keywords, themes, or demographics.

Key Components:

Keywords: Select and manage the keywords that trigger your ads within the ad group. Ensure they are relevant to the ad content and campaign goals.

Ad Copy: Craft ad text or creative elements that align with the keywords and speak directly to the user's search intent.

Bidding: Set bid amounts for the keywords in the ad group to determine how much you're willing to pay for clicks.

Quality Score: Monitor and improve the quality of your ads and landing pages to influence your ad rank and cost per click.

Negative Keywords: Exclude irrelevant search terms to prevent wasted ad spend.

Example: Within the "Summer Shoe Sale" campaign, you can create ad groups for different types of summer shoes, like "Sandals," "Flip-Flops," and "Running Shoes." Each ad group will have its keywords, ad copy, and bid settings tailored to those specific shoe categories.

Effective campaign and ad group management is crucial for optimizing your advertising budget, improving ad relevance, and ultimately achieving your marketing goals. It allows advertisers to target their audience more precisely and deliver a more tailored message to potential customers.

1.6 Introduction to Keyword Targeting :

Keyword targeting is a digital marketing strategy used to reach specific audiences or potential customers based on the keywords they use when searching online. This strategy is commonly employed in search engine marketing (SEM), search engine optimization (SEO), and online advertising campaigns. Here's a more detailed definition:

Keyword Targeting: Keyword targeting involves selecting and focusing on particular keywords or keyword phrases that are relevant to your products, services, or content. These keywords are the terms that your target audience is likely to use when conducting online searches.

The primary objectives of keyword targeting include:

1. **Relevance:** By using keywords relevant to your business or content, you can ensure that your marketing efforts are reaching people who are actively interested in what you offer.

2. **Visibility:** When you optimize your website or create online advertisements around specific keywords, your content is more likely to appear in search engine results when people search for those keywords. This increases your visibility to potential customers.
3. **Traffic:** Keyword targeting can drive organic (unpaid) traffic to your website through SEO or paid traffic through online advertising, which can lead to increased website visitors and potential conversions.
4. **Conversions**: Ultimately, the goal of keyword targeting is to attract individuals who are likely to become customers, subscribers, or engage with your content. By targeting the right keywords, you can increase the likelihood of conversions.

In practice, keyword targeting involves conducting keyword research to identify the most relevant and effective keywords for your specific goals. It also entails optimizing your website content, meta tags, and other on-page elements for these keywords in the case of SEO. For online advertising, it means bidding on or targeting these keywords in ad campaigns to display ads to users searching for those terms.

Keyword targeting is an essential element of online marketing, as it helps businesses connect with their target audience and improve their online visibility and performance

Troubleshooting:

Troubleshooting is a problem-solving process or methodology used to identify, diagnose, and resolve issues, errors, or malfunctions that occur in various systems, devices, or processes. It is commonly employed in fields such as information technology, electronics, mechanics, and many other technical and non-technical areas. The primary goal of troubleshooting is to pinpoint the root cause of a problem and implement effective solutions to restore the system or process to its normal or desired operation.

The troubleshooting process typically involves the following steps:

1. **Problem Identification:** The first step is to identify and define the problem or issue that needs to be addressed. This may involve gathering information about the symptoms, errors, or unexpected behavior of the system or device.
2. **Problem Isolation:** Once the problem is defined, the next step is to isolate and narrow down the potential causes. This might involve testing different components, configurations, or variables to determine the source of the problem.
3. **Root Cause Analysis:** In this step, troubleshooting involves a more in-depth investigation to determine the underlying or root cause of the problem. This may involve examining system logs, conducting tests, or using diagnostic tools.
4. **Solution Development:** Once the root cause is identified, the troubleshooter works on developing one or more solutions to address the problem. These solutions are often based on the analysis of the root cause.
5. **Solution Implementation:** The chosen solution or solutions are put into action to resolve the problem. This may involve making configuration changes, repairing or replacing hardware, or adjusting processes as needed.
6. **Verification and Testing:** After implementing the solution, it is essential to verify that the problem has been

resolved. Testing and monitoring are conducted to ensure that the system or device is functioning correctly.

7. **Documentation**: Troubleshooting efforts and their outcomes are typically documented for future reference. This documentation can be useful for troubleshooting similar issues in the future or for sharing knowledge with others.
8. Troubleshooting can vary in complexity depending on the nature of the problem and the system involved. It is a valuable skill in various professions and everyday life, as it enables individuals to resolve issues and keep systems running smoothly

Questions:

1. Explain keyword Management and Troubleshooting?
2. Define Search Engine Management?
3. Describe about Ad Words?
4. Give a brief Explanation about Google Networks?
5. Illustrate Account Management?
6. Explain Campaign and ad group Management?
7. Relate Account management and group Management?
8. Briefly explain about troubleshooting?
9. Classify ad group management keyword targeting?
10. Briefly explain a Note on Ad Group Management and Explain its Importance ?

CHAPTER - II

2.1 Introduction to SEM Terminologies:

SEM, which stands for Scanning Electron Microscopy, is a powerful imaging technique used in various scientific and industrial applications to visualize the microstructure of materials at high resolution. To better understand SEM terminologies, let's explore some key concepts:

1. **Electron Microscopy (EM):** Electron microscopy is a technique that uses a beam of electrons instead of visible light to magnify and visualize specimens. SEM is a type of electron microscopy.
2. **Electron Beam:** In SEM, an electron beam is generated by an electron source and focused onto the sample. The electrons interact with the sample's surface, resulting in various signals used for imaging.
3. **Cathode:** The source of electrons in an SEM is the cathode. It emits electrons when heated, and these electrons are then accelerated and focused into a fine, focused beam.
4. **Scanning Electron Microscope (SEM):** The instrument used for SEM is known as a scanning electron microscope. It scans the electron beam across the sample's surface to produce high-resolution images.
5. **Specimen:** The sample or specimen is the material or object under examination in the SEM. It can be biological, geological, metallic, or any other type of material.
6. **Secondary Electrons (SE):** When the electron beam strikes the sample, it can dislodge secondary electrons from the sample's surface. Detectors capture these secondary electrons to create high-resolution surface images.

7. **Backscattered Electrons (BSE):** Some electrons are scattered backward when they encounter heavy elements in the sample. BSE detectors capture these electrons, producing images that highlight compositional variations in the sample.
8. **Electron Gun:** The electron gun is responsible for generating and focusing the electron beam that interacts with the specimen.
9. **Electron Detector:** SEMs are equipped with various types of detectors to capture different types of signals. These detectors include secondary electron detectors, backscattered electron detectors, and others for specific applications.
10. **Resolution:** The resolution of an SEM is the ability to distinguish fine details in an image. SEMs are known for their high resolution, enabling the observation of extremely small features on the specimen's surface.
11. **Magnification**: SEMs provide adjustable magnification levels, allowing users to zoom in and out to visualize details at different scales.
12. **Vacuum System:** SEMs operate in a high vacuum environment to prevent electron scattering and ensure the efficient interaction of electrons with the sample.
13. **Stage:** The sample stage holds the specimen and allows precise positioning and movement for imaging different areas of the sample.
14. **SEM Image:** The final output of an SEM is the SEM image, which represents the topographical and/or compositional information of the specimen's surface.
15. **EDS (Energy-Dispersive X-ray Spectroscopy):** EDS is often used in conjunction with SEM to analyze the

elemental composition of the sample. It detects X-rays emitted by the sample when it is bombarded by electrons.

16. **SEM Operator:** The person operating the SEM is responsible for setting imaging parameters, adjusting the instrument, and interpreting the resulting images.

Understanding these SEM terminologies is essential for effectively utilizing scanning electron microscopy in various fields, including materials science, geology, biology, and more. SEM provides invaluable insights into the microstructure and composition of a wide range of materials and samples.

2.2 Pay Per Click (PPC):

Pay-per-click (PPC) is an online advertising model in which advertisers pay a fee each time one of their ads is clicked. It's a way of buying visits to a website rather than attempting to "earn" those visits organically through methods like search engine optimization (SEO).

In a PPC campaign, advertisers bid on specific keywords or phrases relevant to their target audience. When users search for these keywords on search engines or visit websites that display ads, the advertiser's ad may be displayed. If the user clicks on the ad, the advertiser is charged a predetermined fee. The cost per click (CPC) can vary depending on the competitiveness of the keywords and the quality of the ad campaign.

PPC advertising is commonly associated with search engine advertising, such as Google Ads (formerly Google Ad Words), but it can also include advertising on social media platforms and other online advertising networks. This model allows advertisers to control their advertising budget and target specific audiences, making it a popular choice for online marketing.

Types of Pay per Click

Pay-per-click (PPC) is a digital advertising model where advertisers pay a fee each time one of their ads is clicked. There are several types of PPC advertising, each with its unique characteristics. Here are some common PPC types:

1. **Search Advertising:** This is the most well-known form of PPC advertising, where ads appear in search engine results pages (SERPs) like Google, Bing, or Yahoo. Advertisers bid on keywords related to their business, and their ads are displayed when users search for those keywords.
2. **Display Advertising:** Display ads are visual, banner-style ads that appear on websites within a display network. Advertisers can target specific demographics, interests, or websites to display their ads to a relevant audience.
3. **Social Media Advertising:** Popular social media platforms like Facebook, Instagram, Twitter, and LinkedIn offer PPC advertising options. Advertisers can target users based on demographics, interests, and behaviors to display ads in users' social feeds.
4. **Shopping Advertising:** Shopping ads, often used by e-commerce businesses, display product listings with images, prices, and descriptions in search engine results. Google Shopping is a common platform for this type of PPC advertising.

5. **Video Advertising**: Platforms like YouTube provide PPC options for video ads. Advertisers can promote their videos and pay when users watch or interact with the content.
6. **Remarketing / Retargeting:** This strategy involves targeting users who have previously visited your website or interacted with your content. Advertisers use cookies to track user behavior and then display relevant ads to re-engage them.
7. **Mobile Advertising:** Mobile PPC focuses on targeting users on mobile devices, including smartphones and tablets. Advertisers can create mobile-specific ad campaigns to reach this audience.
8. **Local Advertising:** Local PPC aims to target users in a specific geographic area. It's especially valuable for local businesses looking to attract nearby customers. Google Ads and Bing Ads offer options for local targeting.
9. **In-App Advertising:** This form of PPC is used to display ads within mobile apps. Advertisers can choose to display their ads in specific apps, targeting users who are using those apps.
10. **Affiliate Marketing:** Some businesses use PPC advertising to promote affiliate products or services. They pay a commission to affiliates for driving traffic or sales through their PPC ads.
11. **Dynamic Search Ads (DSA):** With DSA, search engines automatically generate ad headlines and landing pages based on the content of your website. This helps advertisers reach a broader audience and ensure that ads are relevant to user searches.

12. **Programmatic Advertising:** Programmatic advertising uses automated technology and algorithms to buy and place ads in real-time auctions, optimizing ad placements based on user data and targeting criteria.

These are some of the most common types of PPC advertising. Advertisers choose the type that aligns best with their business goals and target audience, and they set budgets and bids accordingly to manage their PPC campaigns effectively

2.3 Cost Per Click (CPC):

Cost per Click (CPC) is a digital advertising metric that represents the price an advertiser pays each time a user clicks on their online ad. It is commonly used in pay-per-click (PPC) advertising models, where advertisers are charged a fee for every click their ad receives. CPC is a crucial metric in online advertising campaigns, as it helps advertisers measure the efficiency and effectiveness of their marketing efforts.

CPC is calculated by dividing the total cost of an advertising campaign by the number of clicks generated by the ads. The formula for calculating CPC is:

CPC = Total Cost of Campaign / Number of Clicks

For example, if an advertiser spends $500 on a campaign and the ads receive 1,000 clicks, the CPC for that campaign would be:

CPC = $500 / 1,000 clicks = $0.50 per click

In this case, the advertiser pays 50 cents for each click generated by their ads. CPC can vary widely depending on factors like the industry, platform, targeting options, and competition. Advertisers often set a maximum CPC bid as part of their advertising strategy, which determines the highest amount they are willing to pay for a single click. The actual cost per click an advertiser incurs can be influenced by ad quality, bid competitiveness, and other factors in the auction-based advertising systems used by platforms like Google Ads and Facebook Ads

Types of Cost per Click:

Cost per click (CPC) is a popular online advertising pricing model in which advertisers pay a fee each time a user clicks on one of their ads. There are different types of CPC models and strategies used in online advertising. Here are some common types of CPC:

1. **Standard CPC:** This is the most basic form of CPC advertising. Advertisers set a maximum bid they are willing to pay for a click on their ad. The actual cost per click may vary, but it will not exceed the maximum bid. Search engines and advertising platforms often use this model.
2. **Enhanced CPC (eCPC):** In this model, advertisers allow the advertising platform to adjust their bids for clicks that are more likely to convert into a desired action, such as a sale or a lead. The platform uses historical data and algorithms to make bid adjustments.
3. **Manual CPC:** Advertisers manually set the bid for each keyword or ad group. This offers more control but requires continuous monitoring and adjustments.
4. **Automatic CPC**: Advertisers let the advertising platform automatically set bids to achieve a target cost per conversion or maximize clicks within a set budget. This model relies on machine learning and algorithms.

5. **Adaptive CPC:** This model uses a combination of manual and automatic bidding. Advertisers set maximum CPC bids for some keywords and allow the platform to automatically adjust bids for others.
6. **Bid Modifiers:** Advertisers can adjust their CPC bids based on various factors, such as the user's device, location, time of day, or demographics. For example, they may bid more for clicks from mobile users or for users in specific locations.
7. **Position-Based CPC:** Advertisers set their bids based on the desired ad position on the search engine results page. They may bid higher to secure a top ad placement, or bid lower for lower positions.
8. **Quality Score CPC:** Some platforms, like Google Ads, use a quality score to determine CPC. Advertisers with higher-quality ads may pay lower CPC rates, while those with lower-quality ads may pay more.
9. **Incremental CPC:** Advertisers incrementally increase their bids to ensure their ads appear in higher positions or at specific times when competition is high, such as during a peak shopping season.
10. **Competitive CPC:** Advertisers adjust their bids based on what their competitors are doing. If a competitor raises their bid, the advertiser may choose to increase their bid to remain competitive.
11. **Day parting CPC:** Advertisers set different CPC bids for different times of the day or days of the week based on when their target audience is most active or likely to convert.

12. **Ad Scheduling CPC:** Advertisers can adjust their CPC bids for specific ad schedules, allowing them to bid more during specific date ranges, events, or holidays.

The choice of CPC model depends on an advertiser's goals, budget, and the platform they are using for advertising. Effective CPC management often involves a combination of these models to optimize ad performance.

2.4 Search Engine Results Page (SERP):

A Search Engine Results Page (SERP) is the webpage that a search engine displays in response to a user's query. It's the interface through which users interact with search engines like Google, Bing, or Yahoo to find information, products, services, or answers to their questions. The primary function of a SERP is to present a list of relevant links and information that best match the user's search query.

Here are some key elements typically found on a Search Engine Results Page:

1. **Organic Search Results:** These are the non-paid listings that the search engine deems most relevant to the user's query. They are typically displayed in a list format and include titles, snippets (short descriptions), and URLs. Search engines use complex algorithms to determine the order and ranking of organic search results.
2. **Paid Search Results:** These are the advertisements that appear at the top and sometimes on the side of the SERP. They are labeled as "sponsored" or "ad" and are usually placed there by advertisers who have paid for specific keywords or phrases. These results are often relevant to the user's query but are clearly marked as paid promotions.

3. **Knowledge Graph or Featured Snippets:** Some SERPs include a prominent box or snippet at the top that provides quick answers to the user's query without the need to click on any links. These featured snippets are often derived from trusted sources and aim to provide immediate information.
4. **Images and Video Results:** In addition to text-based listings, SERPs may also include images and video results when the search query is related to visual content. These results can be displayed in a separate section or integrated within the organic listings.
5. **Related Searches:** Many SERPs include a section at the bottom suggesting related or similar search queries, helping users refine or expand their search.
6. **Local Results:** When the user's query has a local intent, such as searching for nearby restaurants or businesses, the SERP may display a map with local listings and reviews.
7. **Shopping Results:** For queries related to products, a dedicated shopping section may appear on the SERP, showcasing products from various online retailers along with prices and links to make purchases.
8. **News and Updates:** SERPs can also feature news articles, blog posts, or other real-time content when the query is related to current events or trending topics.
9. **Pagination and Filters:** Depending on the number of search results, pagination and filtering options may be provided to help users navigate through multiple pages or refine their search criteria.

SERPs are dynamic and continuously evolving, as search engines continually update their algorithms and user interface to enhance the quality and relevance of search results. Understanding how to interpret and optimize for these results is crucial for businesses, marketers, and website owners looking to improve their online visibility and reach a wider audience.

2.5 Click-Through Rate (CTR):

Click-Through Rate (CTR) is a crucial metric used in digital marketing and online advertising to measure the effectiveness of a particular advertising campaign, web page, or digital content. It is a percentage that represents the number of clicks on a specific link, advertisement, or call-to-action (CTA) compared to the number of times that link or ad was shown, often referred to as impressions. CTR is a key indicator of how successful and engaging your online content or advertisements are in motivating users to take the desired action.

Here's how to calculate CTR:

CTR (%) = (Number of Clicks / Number of Impressions) x 100

Key points to understand about CTR:

1. **Measurement of Engagement:** CTR primarily measures the interaction level between your content or ad and your target audience. It indicates how many people found your content compelling enough to click on it.
2. **Benchmarking:** CTR is used to evaluate the performance of different ads, email campaigns, or web pages. By comparing CTRs, marketers can determine which elements are more effective in capturing users' attention.

3. **Higher CTR Indicates Effectiveness:** A higher CTR generally signifies that your content or ad is engaging and relevant to the audience. It can lead to more conversions, such as sales, sign-ups, or other desired actions.
4. **Optimization**: Marketers frequently use CTR data to fine-tune their campaigns. They may experiment with different ad copy, visuals, or targeting strategies to increase CTR and improve their ROI.
5. **Context Matters:** The industry, platform, and audience can greatly influence what is considered a good CTR. What is acceptable in one context may be considered poor in another.
6. **Quality vs. Quantity:** While a high CTR is generally desirable, it's important to consider the quality of the clicks as well. Sometimes, a lower CTR with highly relevant clicks can be more valuable than a high CTR with lots of irrelevant clicks.

CTR is a versatile metric used in various online marketing channels, including search engine advertising (e.g., Google Ads), display advertising, email marketing, and social media advertising. It helps businesses and advertisers understand how well their content resonates with their target audience and provides insights for making data-driven decisions to improve their digital marketing strategies.

2.6 Impression:

Impression can have several different meanings and definitions depending on the context in which it is used. Here are some common meanings:

1. **A Mark or Indentation:** In a physical sense, an impression refers to a mark, dent, or indentation made by pressing or stamping one object onto another. For example, a footprint in the sand or a coin's impression on a piece of paper.
2. **A Feeling or Perception:** In a psychological or sensory context, an impression can refer to a subjective feeling, perception, or belief about something or someone. It's often based on one's observations or interactions. For example, you might have a positive or negative impression of a person after meeting them for the first time.
3. **A Copy or Representation:** An impression can also refer to a copy or representation of something, often produced by a printing or engraving process. For instance, a print of a painting can be called an impression.
4. **Effect or Influence:** In some cases, impression is used to describe the impact, influence, or effect that something has on a person or situation. For example, "The speech left a strong impression on the audience."
5. **A Brief Experience:** It can also refer to a brief encounter or experience, as in "I had the impression that I was being followed."
6. **Marketing and Advertising:** In the context of marketing and advertising, an impression is a measure of the number of times an advertisement is fetched and displayed, regardless of whether it is clicked or not. It is often used to gauge the reach of an online ad campaign.

The specific meaning of "impression" in a given context can vary, so it's important to consider the surrounding words and circumstances to understand its intended definition.

2.7 Split Testing:

Split testing, also known as A/B testing, is a controlled experiment used in marketing, web design, and other fields to evaluate and compare two or more versions of a webpage, email campaign, advertisement, or other digital content to determine which one performs better in terms of a specific goal, such as click-through rate, conversion rate, or user engagement.

Here's a more detailed definition and explanation of split testing:

Definition: Split testing, or A/B testing, is a method of comparing two or more versions (A and B) of a webpage or content to identify which version performs better by measuring specific key performance indicators (KPIs). It involves dividing a website's or campaign's audience into two or more groups and presenting each group with a different variation (A, B, C, etc.) of the content. The goal is to determine which variation leads to higher success metrics, such as more clicks, higher conversion rates, or increased engagement.

Key Components of Split Testing:

1. **Variations:** The different versions of the content you want to test (e.g., two different webpage layouts, two email subject lines, or two ad copy variations).
2. **Randomization:** Participants are assigned randomly to the different variations to ensure that the test results are statistically valid and not influenced by user bias.
3. **Isolation:** Other factors that could affect the outcome (such as the time of day the test is run or external events) should be isolated or controlled for accurate results.

4. **Metrics:** Define the specific metrics or KPIs you want to measure, like click-through rates, conversion rates, bounce rates, or revenue generated.
5. **Sample Size:** Determine the number of users or participants needed for the test to produce statistically significant results.

How Split Testing Works:

1. **Hypothesis:** Start with a hypothesis about what change you want to test. For example, you may hypothesize that a different headline on your webpage will lead to more click-throughs.
2. **Creation of Variations:** Create the variations (A and B) that reflect the change you want to test. For example, you'll create two versions of your webpage with different headlines.
3. **Random Assignment:** Randomly assign users to one of the variations. Some users will see version A, while others will see version B.
4. **Data Collection:** Monitor user interactions and collect data on your chosen metrics for both variations over a set period.
5. **Analysis:** Analyze the data to determine which variation outperformed the other(s) in terms of the defined metrics.
6. **Implementation:** Implement the winning variation (the one that produced better results) as the default or desired version for your audience.
7. **Continuous Testing:** Split testing is an ongoing process. You can continually test and refine different elements of your content to optimize performance.

Split testing is a valuable tool for optimizing digital content and marketing strategies because it allows data-driven decision-making. By comparing different versions of content, organizations can make informed choices that lead to improved user engagement and ultimately better business outcomes

2.8 Development of PPC ads:

PPC, or Pay-Per-Click, ads are a form of online advertising where advertisers pay a fee each time their ad is clicked by a user. The development of PPC ads refers to the process of creating and managing these ads to achieve specific marketing or business goals. This process typically involves the following steps:

1. **Goal Definition:** The first step in developing PPC ads is to clearly define your advertising goals. This could be increasing website traffic, generating leads, boosting sales, or raising brand awareness.
2. **Keyword Research:** Identify the keywords and phrases that are relevant to your business and that your target audience is likely to use in their online searches. These keywords will be the foundation of your PPC campaigns.
3. **Campaign Setup:** Create a PPC campaign on the advertising platform of your choice (e.g., Google Ads, Microsoft Advertising, Facebook Ads). This involves setting your budget, targeting options, and ad schedule.
4. **Ad Creation:** Develop compelling ad copy that is relevant to the chosen keywords. The ad should be engaging and encourage users to click. You may also need to create visual elements like images or videos for display ads.

5. **Landing Page Optimization:** Ensure that the landing page users are directed to after clicking the ad is relevant to the ad's content and provides a good user experience. This can impact your ad's Quality Score and ad rank.
6. **Bid Management:** Set your maximum bid for each keyword or ad group. This determines how much you're willing to pay for a click. Effective bid management is crucial for controlling costs and getting the desired results.
7. **Ad Testing:** Conduct A/B testing to compare different ad variations and determine which ones perform best. This can involve testing different headlines, ad copy, and visual elements.
8. **Monitoring and Analysis:** Continuously monitor the performance of your PPC ads. Use analytics and reporting tools to track key metrics like click-through rate (CTR), conversion rate, and return on ad spend (ROAS).
9. **Optimization:** Based on the data you gather from monitoring, make adjustments to your campaigns to improve their performance. This may involve adjusting bids, refining targeting, or modifying ad content.
10. **Scaling**: If your PPC campaigns are achieving your goals and providing a positive return on investment, you can consider increasing your budget and expanding your advertising efforts.
11. **Compliance and Quality Control:** Ensure that your ads comply with the advertising platform's policies and guidelines to avoid ad disapprovals or account suspensions.
12. **Regular Reporting:** Share performance reports with stakeholders and make data-driven decisions for future campaigns.

The development of PPC ads is an ongoing process, and success requires continuous refinement and adaptation based on the changing competitive landscape and evolving user behavior. Effective PPC management can help businesses reach their target audience and drive desired actions while managing advertising costs.

2.9 CPM and CPA Campaigns :

CPM and CPA are two different pricing models used in online advertising campaigns. They determine how advertisers pay for the placement and performance of their ads.

1. **CPM (Cost Per Mille):** CPM stands for "Cost Per Mille," where "mille" is Latin for a thousand. In a CPM advertising campaign, advertisers pay for every 1,000 impressions (views) of their ad. Impressions refer to how many times an ad is displayed to a user, regardless of whether the user interacts with it or takes any specific action. CPM is typically used for brand awareness and exposure campaigns, where the primary goal is to get the ad in front of as many eyeballs as possible.

   The formula for calculating the cost in a CPM campaign is:
   Cost = (Total Impressions / 1,000) x CPM rate
2. **CPA (Cost Per Acquisition):** CPA stands for "Cost Per Acquisition" or "Cost Per Action." In a CPA advertising campaign, advertisers pay for a specific action that a user takes as a result of clicking on their ad. The action could be a purchase, a form submission, a sign-up, or any other predefined conversion goal. Unlike CPM, where you pay for impressions, in a CPA campaign, you pay only when a user completes the desired action. This model is often

used for performance-oriented campaigns, as advertisers are guaranteed a specific outcome for their spending.

The formula for calculating the cost in a CPA campaign is:

Cost = Total Cost / Number of Conversions

CPM and CPA campaigns serve different objectives. CPM is used when the goal is to get your ad in front of as many people as possible, without necessarily focusing on user actions. CPA, on the other hand, is used when the primary objective is to drive specific user actions, and advertisers are willing to pay based on the achievement of those actions.

Advertisers typically choose between CPM and CPA based on their campaign goals, target audience, and the nature of their products or services. Additionally, there are other pricing models, such as CPC (Cost Per Click), which falls between CPM and CPA, where advertisers pay for each click on their ad, regardless of whether the user completes the desired action.

Questions:

1. Summarize about SEM Technologies?
2. Tell about Pay Per click (PPC)?
3. How does PPC differ from other online advertising models, such as CPM (Cost Per Mille) or CPA (Cost Per Acquisition)?
4. How do you set a budget for a PPC campaign, and what factors should be considered?
5. How can you optimize ad copy for better click-through rates (CTR)?
6. What is the role of landing pages in a PPC campaign, and how can they be optimized for better performance?

7. Quote Search Engine Result Page?
8. Define the Features of SEM? And explain briefly ?
9. What is mean by Search Engine Optimization?
10. Explain the significance and features of SEO?
11. What is mean by CPM and CPA campaigns and Design about search engine result page?

CHAPTER – III

3.1 Retargeting:

Retargeting, also known as remarketing, is a digital advertising strategy used by businesses and marketers to re-engage with potential customers who have previously interacted with their brand or website but did not complete a desired action, such as making a purchase, signing up for a newsletter, or filling out a contact form. The main goal of retargeting is to remind these visitors of your products or services and encourage them to return and convert.

Here's a more detailed definition and explanation of retargeting:

Definition: Retargeting is a form of online advertising that targets individuals who have shown some level of interest in a brand or website by tracking their online behavior. It involves displaying relevant ads to these individuals as they browse other websites or social media platforms, reminding them of the brand and encouraging them to take the desired action.

How Retargeting Works:

1. **Visitor Interaction:** A user visits a website, browses products, services, or content, but does not complete the desired action, such as making a purchase.
2. **Tracking Cookies:** When the user visits the website, a tracking cookie is placed in their browser. This cookie stores information about their visit, such as the pages they viewed or the products they added to a shopping cart.

3. **Ad Placement:** As the user continues to browse the internet, retargeting technology identifies them based on the tracking cookie and displays targeted ads related to the products or content they showed interest in. These ads can appear on various websites and social media platforms.
4. **Encouraging Conversion:** The goal of these ads is to remind the user about the brand or products and encourage them to return to the website and complete the desired action. These ads can be customized to create a sense of urgency or offer discounts to entice the user.

Benefits of Retargeting:

- **Increased Conversions:** Retargeting can boost conversion rates by reminding users of products or services they've shown interest in.
- **Improved Brand Recall:** It helps reinforce brand awareness and keeps the brand in the minds of potential customers.
- **Precise Targeting:** Advertisers can segment their audience and create highly targeted campaigns.
- **Cost-Effective:** Since it targets users who have already shown interest, it can be more cost-effective than broad advertising.

It's important to note that retargeting should be used judiciously to avoid overwhelming users with ads, which can lead to negative reactions. It should be part of a broader digital marketing strategy and should respect privacy and data protection regulations.

3.2 Comparison between SEO and SEM :

SEO (Search Engine Optimization) and SEM (Search Engine Marketing) are two distinct online marketing strategies used to improve a website's visibility on search engine results pages (SERPs). While both aim to increase website traffic and enhance online presence, they employ different techniques and have unique characteristics. Here's a comparison between SEO and SEM:

1. **Definition**:
    - **SEO:** SEO is the practice of optimizing a website's content, structure, and various on-page and off-page elements to improve its organic (unpaid) search engine rankings. It focuses on enhancing the website's visibility in natural search results.
    - **SEM:** SEM is a broader term encompassing various paid advertising strategies to promote a website within search engine results. It includes both paid search advertising (PPC - Pay-Per-Click) and organic SEO efforts.

2. **Traffic Source**:
    - **SEO:** Generates organic traffic, which is free and obtained through improving the website's relevance and authority to search engines.
    - **SEM:** Generates paid traffic through advertising. Advertisers pay for each click or impression, depending on the advertising model used.

3. **Cost**:
   - **SEO:** While there are costs associated with optimizing a website for SEO, such as hiring SEO professionals or creating quality content, the primary traffic generated through SEO is organic and doesn't incur per-click costs.
   - **SEM:** SEM involves direct advertising costs, as you pay for each click (PPC) or impression (CPI - Cost Per Impression) depending on your campaign.

4. **Speed of Results**:
   - **SEO:** It can take time to see significant results with SEO. It often requires months for changes to impact search engine rankings.
   - **SEM:** SEM can generate immediate results. Once you set up an ad campaign, your website can appear at the top of search results, potentially driving traffic right away.

5. **Sustainability**:
   - **SEO:** When properly executed, SEO can provide long-term benefits and sustainable organic traffic, even after initial optimization efforts.
   - **SEM:** The traffic generated through SEM is short-term and dependent on your advertising budget. When you stop the ad campaigns, your visibility decreases.

6. **Control**:
   - **SEO:** You have less direct control over your rankings because they depend on search engine algorithms. SEO is about optimizing your website to align with these algorithms.

- **SEM:** SEM offers more control, as you can adjust your ad campaigns in real-time, including targeting, keywords, and budget.

7. **Keyword Targeting**:
   - **SEO:** SEO involves optimizing your content around specific keywords to improve your website's relevance to those search terms.
   - **SEM:** SEM allows you to bid on and target specific keywords directly in your advertising campaigns.

In summary, SEO and SEM serve different purposes, with SEO focusing on organic, unpaid traffic and SEM encompassing paid advertising efforts. Your choice between the two depends on your specific goals, budget, timeline, and desired level of control over your online marketing efforts. In many cases, businesses use a combination of both SEO and SEM to maximize their online visibility and reach.

3.3 SEO: Understanding Search Engine Optimization:

Search Engine Optimization (SEO) is a multifaceted digital marketing discipline and set of strategies aimed at enhancing a website's visibility and ranking in search engine results pages (SERPs). The primary objective of SEO is to increase the organic (non-paid) traffic to a website by optimizing various on-page and off-page elements to make the site more relevant, authoritative, and user-friendly in the eyes of search engines like Google, Bing, and Yahoo.

Key components of SEO include:

1. **Keyword Research**: Identifying and selecting the right keywords or phrases that users commonly search for in relation to your content, products, or services.

2. **On-Page Optimization:** Refining the content, HTML, and other on-page elements of a website to ensure that it is relevant and well-structured for search engines.
3. **Off-Page Optimization**: Building high-quality backlinks from authoritative websites to boost a site's credibility and authority.
4. **Technical SEO**: Ensuring the website is technically sound, with factors like fast loading times, mobile-friendliness, and a secure HTTPS connection.
5. **Content Creation**: Developing high-quality, informative, and engaging content that satisfies the needs and interests of your target audience.
6. **User Experience (UX):** Enhancing the overall user experience by optimizing site navigation, improving load times, and making the website easy to use on various devices.
7. **Analytics and Monitoring:** Constantly measuring and analyzing the effectiveness of SEO efforts through tools like Google Analytics to make data-driven improvements.

SEO is an ongoing process, as search engines frequently update their algorithms to deliver more relevant results to users. As such, website owners and digital marketers must adapt and refine their SEO strategies over time to maintain or improve their search engine rankings and increase their online visibility. Successful SEO can lead to increased organic traffic, higher conversions, and improved online visibility, all of which can contribute to the success of an online business or website.

3.4 Features of SEO:

Search Engine Optimization (SEO) encompasses a wide range of techniques and strategies aimed at improving a website's visibility and ranking in search engine results pages (SERPs). These features or elements of SEO work together to enhance a website's online presence and drive organic traffic.

Here are some of the key features of SEO:

1. **On-Page SEO:**

- **Content Optimization:** Creating high-quality, relevant, and engaging content with the right keywords and structure.
- **Keyword Research:** Identifying the most relevant and high-traffic keywords for your industry or niche.
- **Title Tags and Meta Descriptions:** Crafting compelling and keyword-rich titles and descriptions for web pages.
- **Header Tags**: Properly structuring content with H1, H2, and H3 tags.
- **Image Optimization:** Adding descriptive alt tags to images for better accessibility and SEO.
- **URL Structure:** Creating clean, user-friendly URLs that include relevant keywords.
- **Internal Linking:** Linking to other pages within your website to improve navigation and distribute link equity.
- **Page Speed Optimization:** Ensuring fast-loading web pages for better user experience and SEO rankings.

2. **Off-Page SEO:**

- **Link Building:** Acquiring high-quality, relevant backlinks from reputable websites to boost authority and rankings.

- **Social Media Engagement:** Building a strong social media presence and encouraging social signals.
- **Online Reputation Management:** Monitoring and managing your online reputation to enhance trust and credibility.

3. **Technical SEO:**

- **Mobile-Friendliness:** Ensuring that your website is responsive and user-friendly on mobile devices.
- **Site Speed:** Optimizing website performance for faster loading times.
- **XML Sitemaps:** Creating and submitting sitemaps to search engines for better crawling and indexing.
- **Robots.txt:** Implementing robots.txt files to control search engine crawler access.
- **Canonical Tags:** Preventing duplicate content issues by specifying canonical URLs.
- **Schema Markup:** Adding structured data to provide context to search engines about your content.

4. **User Experience (UX):**

- **User-Friendly Design:** Creating a visually appealing, easy-to-navigate website.
- **Mobile Optimization:** Ensuring a seamless user experience on mobile devices.
- **Secure and Accessible:** Implementing SSL certificates for security and ensuring accessibility for all users.

5. **Content Quality:**

- **Originality:** Avoiding duplicate or plagiarized content.
- **Relevance:** Creating content that matches user intent and needs.

- **Authority:** Demonstrating expertise and trustworthiness in your field.

6. **Analytics and Monitoring:**

- **Web Analytics:** Using tools like Google Analytics to track website performance and user behavior.
- **Keyword Ranking Tracking:** Monitoring keyword rankings in search results.
- **SEO Audits:** Periodically evaluating and optimizing your SEO strategy.

7. **Local SEO (for businesses with physical locations):**

- **Google My Business:** Optimizing your Google My Business listing.
- **Local Citations:** Ensuring consistent business information across the web.
- **Customer Reviews:** Encouraging and managing customer reviews.

8. **Algorithm Updates:**

- Staying informed about search engine algorithm changes and adapting your SEO strategies accordingly.

SEO is an ongoing process, and the features mentioned above should be continuously monitored and adjusted to maintain and improve your website's search engine rankings and visibility.

3.5 Significance of SEO :

SEO, or Search Engine Optimization, is a critical aspect of digital marketing and online presence. Its significance cannot be overstated, and it plays a pivotal role in the success of websites and online businesses. Here are some of the key reasons why SEO is significant:

1. **Improved Visibility**: SEO helps your website rank higher in search engine results pages (SERPs). When your website appears at the top of the search results for relevant keywords, it is more likely to be seen by users, which increases your online visibility.
2. **Increased Organic Traffic**: High search engine rankings lead to more organic (non-paid) traffic. This traffic is often more valuable because it consists of users actively searching for information, products, or services related to your business.
3. **Cost-Effective Marketing:** Compared to paid advertising, SEO is a cost-effective long-term strategy. While it requires an initial investment, the ongoing costs are relatively low, and the benefits can compound over time.
4. **Credibility and Trust:** Websites that rank well in search results are often perceived as more credible and trustworthy by users. A strong SEO strategy can help establish your brand's authority in your industry.
5. **User Experience:** SEO is not just about optimizing for search engines; it's also about improving the user experience on your website. By creating a well-structured, user-friendly site, you can engage visitors and keep them coming back.
6. **Competitive Advantage**: Your competitors are likely investing in SEO, so it's essential to keep up or surpass them in search engine rankings. Staying ahead in the search results can give you a competitive edge.

7. **Targeted Traffic:** SEO allows you to target specific keywords and demographics, ensuring that you reach your ideal audience. This means that the traffic you attract is more likely to convert into customers.
8. **Analytics and Data**: SEO provides valuable data and insights about user behavior and preferences. This information can be used to refine your marketing strategies and make data-driven decisions.
9. **Global Reach**: SEO can help you reach a global audience, expanding your market and customer base far beyond your local or regional reach.
10. **Adaptation to Mobile and Voice Search**: With the increasing use of mobile devices and voice-activated search, SEO helps you optimize your online presence for these evolving search methods.
11. **Long-Term Growth**: A well-executed SEO strategy can deliver long-term benefits, as your website's authority and search rankings continue to improve over time.
12. **Measurable Results**: SEO is highly measurable, allowing you to track the impact of your efforts and adjust your strategy as needed.

In summary, SEO is significant because it helps websites and businesses increase their visibility, attract targeted traffic, build credibility, and achieve long-term growth in a cost-effective manner. It's an essential component of any successful online presence and digital marketing strategy.

3.6 Inverted Pyramid in SEO:

In the context of SEO (Search Engine Optimization), the "inverted pyramid" is not a commonly used term or concept.

However, the inverted pyramid structure is a traditional approach in journalism and writing that may have some relevance in content creation for SEO. Here's an explanation of the inverted pyramid structure and how it might be applied to SEO:

1. **Inverted Pyramid Structure in Journalism:** The inverted pyramid is a writing style where the most important information is presented at the beginning of an article or story, followed by details of decreasing importance. This structure is used to ensure that readers get the key information immediately, even if they only read the first few sentences or paragraphs. It helps to engage readers quickly and is often associated with news articles.
2. **Application to SEO:** In the context of SEO, the inverted pyramid structure can be used to optimize the content on a webpage for search engines and user experience. Here's how it might apply:
   - **Keyword Placement:** Place your primary target keyword and essential information in the first paragraph or near the beginning of the content. Search engines pay close attention to the initial content on a page.
   - **Content Hierarchy:** Organize your content with the most critical information or main points at the top, followed by supporting details. This makes it easier for both users and search engine crawlers to understand the main topic of the page.
   - **Readability and User Engagement:** By providing valuable information upfront, you can engage users and potentially reduce bounce rates (the percentage of visitors who leave a page quickly). Engaged users are more likely to stay on your page and explore further.

- **Meta Description:** Craft a clear and enticing meta description for your page, which is the snippet that appears in search engine results. This is an opportunity to summarize your content and entice users to click through.
- **Heading Structure:** Use a hierarchical heading structure (H1, H2, H3, etc.) to organize your content. The main topic should be in the H1 tag, followed by subtopics in H2 and H3 tags. Search engines use this structure to understand the content's hierarchy.

While the concept of the inverted pyramid is not explicitly an SEO strategy, its principles of presenting important information first and organizing content for readability and user engagement can be valuable for SEO efforts. It ensures that both users and search engines can quickly grasp the core message and intent of your content.

Questions:

1. What are the key metrics to monitor when implementing a retargeting campaign within the context of SEO?
2. What tools or platforms are effective for implementing SEO-focused retargeting campaigns?
3. How does retargeting impact user experience on my website, and what steps can I take to ensure it enhances rather than hinders the user journey?
4. Briefly Explain about the Comparison between SEO and SEM?
5. How do search engines work, and how does SEO help in improving a website's ranking?

6. Explain the difference between white hat and black hat SEO. Why is it important to follow ethical SEO practices?
7. Explain the concept of SEO audits and their importance.?
8. How does voice search impact SEO strategies, and what adjustments should be made to accommodate it?
9. What are the common SEO mistakes that businesses make, and how can they be avoided?
10. Explain the importance of creating an XML sitemap for a website.?

CHAPTER – IV

4.1 On Page SEO Meaning:

On-page SEO, which stands for "on-page search engine optimization," refers to the practices and strategies used to optimize individual web pages on a website in order to improve their visibility and ranking in search engine results pages (SERPs). The goal of on-page SEO is to make web pages more attractive and relevant to both search engines and users. It involves various factors, including content, HTML source code, and the overall structure of a webpage. Here are some key aspects of on-page SEO:

1. **Content:** Creating high-quality, valuable, and relevant content is crucial for on-page SEO. This includes using target keywords strategically, providing well-structured and informative content, and addressing the needs and interests of the target audience.
2. **Title Tags**: Title tags are HTML elements that define the title of a web page. Optimizing title tags with relevant keywords can improve the page's search engine ranking.
3. **Meta Descriptions**: Meta descriptions are brief summaries of a web page's content that appear in search engine results. Crafting compelling meta descriptions can encourage users to click on your link.
4. **Header Tags:** Header tags (H1, H2, H3, etc.) structure the content on a webpage and help search engines understand the hierarchy and relevance of different sections.
5. **URL Structure:** Creating clean, concise, and descriptive URLs can improve the user experience and make it easier for search engines to index your content.

6. **Keyword Optimization**: Research and use relevant keywords within your content, but avoid keyword stuffing, as search engines penalize excessive use of keywords.
7. **Image Optimization**: Optimize images by using descriptive filenames and adding alt tags. This helps with both SEO and accessibility.
8. **Internal Linking**: Strategically link to other relevant pages on your website to improve navigation and distribute link equity.
9. **Mobile Friendliness**: Ensure that your web pages are mobile-responsive, as Google and other search engines prioritize mobile-friendly websites.
10. **Page Speed**: Fast-loading pages are preferred by both users and search engines. Optimize your website's performance to improve SEO.
11. **User Experience**: A good user experience, including easy navigation, readable content, and minimal pop-ups or interstitials, can positively impact your SEO.
12. **Social Sharing:** Make it easy for users to share your content on social media, which can indirectly influence SEO.
13. **Schema Markup**: Implement structured data markup to provide search engines with additional context about your content, which can lead to rich snippets in search results.

On-page SEO is an essential part of a broader SEO strategy, which also includes off-page SEO (external factors like backlinks) and technical SEO (site structure, indexing, and other technical elements). When done effectively, on-page SEO can help improve your website's visibility in search results, drive organic traffic, and enhance the overall user experience.

Definition of On Page SEO :

Search Engine Optimization (SEO) is a set of practices and strategies aimed at improving a website's visibility and ranking on search engine results pages (SERPs). The primary goal of SEO is to increase organic (non-paid) traffic to a website by optimizing its content, structure, and other elements to make it more appealing to search engines like Google, Bing, and Yahoo.

Key aspects of SEO include:

1. **Keyword Research**: Identifying the keywords and phrases that users commonly search for and that are relevant to your website's content. These keywords are then strategically integrated into the website's content.
2. **On-Page Optimization**: This involves optimizing the content on individual web pages, including using target keywords in titles, headings, meta descriptions, and body text. It also involves improving the overall user experience, site speed, and mobile-friendliness.
3. **Off-Page Optimization**: This includes building high-quality backlinks to your website from reputable sources. Backlinks are an important factor in search engine rankings, as they can demonstrate the credibility and authority of your website.
4. **Technical SEO**: Technical aspects of a website, such as its site structure, page load times, mobile optimization, and secure connections (HTTPS), play a significant role in SEO. Ensuring a website is technically sound is crucial for search engine visibility.
5. **Content Quality**: High-quality, informative, and engaging content is essential for SEO. Search engines aim to provide

users with valuable and relevant information, so creating content that meets these criteria is crucial.

6. **User Experience**: A positive user experience, including easy navigation and a well-designed site layout, can lead to higher user engagement and better SEO rankings.
7. **Local SEO**: If your business has a physical location or serves a local audience, optimizing for local search is essential. This includes creating and optimizing Google My Business listings and ensuring consistent NAP (Name, Address, Phone) information across the web.
8. **Analytics and Monitoring**: Regularly monitoring website performance through tools like Google Analytics and Search Console is crucial for understanding the effectiveness of your SEO efforts. This data can help in making adjustments and improvements.

SEO is an ongoing process, as search engines frequently update their algorithms. Website owners and marketers need to adapt and refine their strategies to maintain or improve their search engine rankings. It's also important to note that ethical and "white hat" SEO practices are recommended, as attempts to manipulate search results through spammy or unethical tactics can lead to penalties and a decrease in search visibility.

4.2 KEYWORD research and Keyword Planner:

Keyword research is a crucial aspect of search engine optimization (SEO) and online marketing. Google's Keyword Planner is a tool within Google Ads that can help you find relevant keywords for your website or online content. Here's how to perform keyword research using Google Keyword Planner:

1. **Access Google Keyword Planner:**
   - Go to Google Ads (https://ads.google.com) and log in with your Google account.
   - Click on "Tools & Settings" in the upper right corner.
   - Under the "Planning" section, select "Keyword Planner."
2. **Choose Your Goal:**
   - Keyword Planner offers two main options: "Find new keywords" and "Get search volume and forecasts." Choose the one that best aligns with your goals.
3. **Enter Seed Keywords:**
   - In the "Find new keywords" option, start by entering one or more seed keywords or phrases related to your content, product, or topic.
4. **Targeting Settings:**
   - Specify your targeting options. You can select location, language, and other preferences to narrow down your results.
5. **Get Keyword Ideas:**
   - Click "Get Results" to see a list of keyword ideas related to your seed keywords. You'll get information on search volume, competition, and other metrics.
6. **Filter and Sort:**
   - You can filter and sort the keyword ideas based on various criteria such as search volume, competition, and suggested bid. This helps you identify the most relevant keywords for your campaign.
7. **Review Keyword Data:**
   - Click on individual keywords to see more details, including historical trends, average monthly searches, and the competition level.

8. **Add Keywords to a Plan:**
- Once you've identified relevant keywords, you can add them to a plan. This is helpful if you want to create a campaign using Google Ads, but it's not necessary if you're only doing research.

9. **Download Keyword Data:**
- You can also download the keyword data for offline analysis or to share with your team.

10. **Refine Your List:**
- Review your selected keywords and remove any that aren't relevant to your content or campaign goals. Focus on high-value, highly relevant keywords.

11. **Create Content and Optimize:**
- Use the selected keywords to create content or optimize existing content on your website. Make sure to use keywords naturally and provide value to your audience.

12. **Monitor and Adjust:**
- Continuously monitor the performance of your keywords using tools like Google Analytics. Adjust your strategy based on the results and adapt to changes in search trends.

Remember that while Google Keyword Planner is a valuable tool, it's just one part of comprehensive SEO and content marketing strategy. Combine it with other research methods and stay updated on industry trends to remain competitive in the online landscape.

Keyword research is a crucial part of SEO and digital marketing. Google Keyword Planner is a free tool offered by Google Ads that can help you find relevant keywords for your website or content. Here are some notes on how to perform keyword research using Google Keyword Planner:

1. **Access Google Keyword Planner**:
- You need a Google Ads account to use Keyword Planner. Create one if you don't have it already.
- Sign in to your Google Ads account and go to the "Tools & Settings" menu. Under "Planning," you'll find "Keyword Planner."
2. **Select the Right Tool**:
- Keyword Planner offers two main tools: "Discover new keywords" and "Get search volume and forecasts." Choose the appropriate one for your research.
3. **Discover New Keywords**:
- If you're starting from scratch, select "Discover new keywords."
- Enter a product or service related to your business or content.
4. **Refine Your Search**:
- You can specify targeting options like location, language, and search network.
- Adjust the date range for historical data or forecasts.
5. **Review Keyword Ideas**:
- Keyword Planner will provide a list of keyword ideas related to your input.
- Analyze the keywords for relevance and search volume. Focus on keywords with high search volume and relevance to your content.
6. **Filter and Sort Keywords**:
- Use filters to narrow down the keyword list based on criteria like search volume, competition, and keyword text.
- Sort the keywords by different parameters to prioritize your target keywords.

7. **Analyze Competition**:
- Check the competition level for each keyword. High competition might make it difficult to rank for that keyword.

8. **Keyword Forecasts**:
- If you select "Get search volume and forecasts," you can get estimated traffic and bid data for your keywords.

9. **Keyword Groups**:
- Group related keywords together to create targeted content around specific themes.

10. **Export Data**:
- Once you've selected your keywords, you can export the data as a CSV file for further analysis or integration with other tools.

11. **Use Negative Keywords**:
- Consider negative keywords to filter out irrelevant traffic. These are words you don't want to trigger your ads.

12. **Regularly Update Your Research**:
- Keyword trends change over time, so it's essential to keep your research up to date and adjust your content strategy accordingly.

13. **Plan Your Content**:
- Once you've identified your target keywords, plan your content around them. Include them naturally in your webpages, articles, or ads.

14. **Track and Analyze Performance**:
- Use tools like Google Analytics to monitor the performance of your content and the keywords that are driving traffic and conversions.

Remember that keyword research is an ongoing process, and staying up to date with the latest trends and changes in search behavior is crucial for maintaining and improving your online presence.

Definition & Overview:

Google Keyword Planner is a tool provided by Google within their Google Ads platform (formerly known as Google AdWords). It is primarily designed for advertisers and website owners to conduct keyword research and plan their advertising campaigns. Keyword research is a crucial part of search engine optimization (SEO) and pay-per-click (PPC) advertising.

Here's a definition and an overview of how Google Keyword Planner works:

1. **Keyword Research**: Google Keyword Planner helps users discover relevant keywords and phrases that people are searching for on Google. This tool is especially useful for understanding what keywords to target in your content or advertising campaigns.
2. **Search Volume**: It provides information about the average monthly search volume for specific keywords, helping you gauge the popularity of a particular keyword.
3. **Keyword Suggestions**: Google Keyword Planner offers keyword suggestions related to your initial query. This can help you discover additional keywords that might be relevant to your topic.
4. **Competition Analysis**: It provides insight into the level of competition for specific keywords, indicating how many advertisers are bidding on those keywords in Google Ads.

This can be useful in assessing the competitiveness of keywords.

5. **Cost-Per-Click (CPC) Estimates**: For PPC advertisers, Google Keyword Planner offers estimated CPC values, giving you an idea of how much you might need to bid in order to compete for a particular keyword in advertising auctions.
6. **Historical Data**: You can also access historical data, allowing you to see how a keyword's search volume and competition have changed over time.
7. **Geographic Targeting**: Google Keyword Planner lets you specify geographic locations to see keyword data that's relevant to your target audience.
8. **Filtering and Sorting**: You can filter and sort keywords based on various criteria, making it easier to identify the most relevant and valuable keywords for your purposes.
9. **Export Data**: You can download keyword data for later reference or analysis.

To use Google Keyword Planner, you'll typically need a Google Ads account, as it's primarily intended for advertisers. However, you can access certain keyword data without running ads by setting up a campaign without actually spending money.

Keyword research is essential for improving your website's visibility on search engines, attracting organic traffic, and optimizing your online advertising efforts. Google Keyword Planner is a valuable tool for this purpose, whether you're an advertiser or a content creator looking to improve your SEO.

4.3 Difference between keyword Stuffing & KW Placement :

Keyword stuffing and keyword placement are two distinct approaches to using keywords in digital content, especially in the context of search engine optimization (SEO). Let's explore the key differences between them:

1. **Keyword Stuffing**:

- **Overuse of Keywords**: Keyword stuffing involves excessively and unnaturally inserting keywords into a piece of content, with the primary goal of manipulating search engine rankings. This often results in a high keyword density, where the keyword is repeated far more often than it naturally fits in the text.
- **Poor User Experience**: Keyword stuffing can make content read poorly and disrupt the natural flow of the text. It can be annoying and confusing to readers, leading to a poor user experience.
- **Search Engine Penalties**: Search engines, like Google, have algorithms that can detect keyword stuffing. When detected, websites may be penalized with lower rankings or even be removed from search engine results.
- **Outdated and Ineffective**: Search engines have become much more sophisticated, and keyword stuffing is an outdated and ineffective strategy. Modern SEO values high-quality, user-friendly content.

2. **Keyword Placement**:

- **Strategic Use of Keywords**: Keyword placement involves strategically incorporating keywords into content in a natural and relevant manner. It focuses on optimizing content for search engines while maintaining a good user experience.

- **Content Relevance**: In keyword placement, the emphasis is on ensuring that keywords are used in a way that's contextually relevant to the content's topic and purpose.
- **User-Friendly**: Content optimized through keyword placement is more user-friendly and easier to read because the keywords are seamlessly integrated into the text.
- **Effective SEO Strategy**: Keyword placement is considered an effective SEO strategy in the current landscape. It ensures that search engines can understand what the content is about without compromising the user experience.

In summary, keyword stuffing is an outdated and frowned-upon practice that involves excessive and unnatural keyword repetition to manipulate search engine rankings, while keyword placement is a more modern and effective approach that strategically incorporates keywords into content in a natural and relevant manner to enhance both search engine visibility and user experience. It's important for digital marketers and content creators to adopt the latter strategy to achieve long-term SEO success.

4.4 Selection of a Domain Name :

The selection of a domain name refers to the process of choosing and registering a unique and user-friendly web address for a website. A domain name is a crucial part of a website's identity on the internet, and it plays a significant role in how users find and remember a particular website. Here's a more detailed definition of the elements involved in selecting a domain name:

1. **Unique Identity**: A domain name should be distinctive and not already in use by another website. It's essential to

choose a name that reflects your brand, business, or the content of your website.

2. **User-Friendly**: The domain name should be easy to remember and type. Short, simple, and descriptive names are often more effective. Avoid using complex spellings, hyphens, or special characters that can confuse users.
3. **Relevance**: Ideally, your domain name should be relevant to the content or purpose of your website. This helps users understand what your site is about and can improve search engine optimization (SEO).
4. **Domain Extension**: The domain extension, also known as a top-level domain (TLD), is the part of the domain name that comes after the dot (e.g., .com, .org, .net). Choose an extension that best suits your website's purpose. Common TLDs like .com are generally a safe choice, but there are many other options available.
5. **Branding**: Your domain name can be an important part of your brand identity. It should align with your brand name or be closely associated with it to reinforce your online presence.
6. **Avoid Trademark Issues**: Ensure that your chosen domain name does not infringe on any trademarks or copyrights. Using someone else's trademarked name could lead to legal issues.
7. **Keywords**: Including relevant keywords in your domain name can help with SEO and make it more discoverable in search engine results. However, it's important not to overstuff your domain name with keywords, as this can make it less user-friendly.
8. **Domain Registrar**: To acquire a domain name, you need to register it through a domain registrar, a company or

organization authorized to manage domain registrations. Choose a reputable registrar that provides good customer support and transparent pricing.

9. **Renewal Considerations**: Keep in mind that domain names require annual renewal. Make sure you understand the renewal process and associated costs to avoid losing your domain.
10. **Future-Proofing**: Think about the long-term implications of your domain name. Will it still be relevant and effective several years from now?

When selecting a domain name, it's a good practice to brainstorm multiple options, seek feedback from others, and consider the factors mentioned above to make an informed choice that suits your website's purpose and goals. Once you've decided on a domain name, you can proceed to register it with a domain registrar to establish your online presence.

4.5 Page Naming and Folder Image Naming :

Naming pages, folders, and images on a website or in a digital file system is important for organization and user-friendliness. Here are some guidelines for naming these elements effectively:

1. Page Naming:

When naming website pages, consider the following:

- Use descriptive and concise titles: Page names should reflect the content or purpose of the page. Avoid vague or generic names.
- Use hyphens or underscores: To separate words in a page name, it's common to use hyphens (e.g., "about-us" or "contact-page") or underscores (e.g., "about_us" or "contact_page"). Avoid using spaces or special characters.

- Keep it lowercase: Use lowercase letters for consistency and to prevent confusion (e.g., "products" instead of "Products").
- Be consistent: Maintain a consistent naming convention across your website to make it easier for users and developers to navigate.

2. Folder Naming:

When organizing files or content into folders, follow these principles:

- Use descriptive names: Folders should have clear and relevant names that reflect the content they contain. For example, a folder containing images for a blog might be named "blog-images."
- Use hyphens or underscores: Similar to page naming, separate words with hyphens or underscores.
- Keep it organized: Create a logical folder structure to help users and collaborators find files easily. For example, you could have separate folders for images, documents, scripts, etc.

4.6 Image Naming:

Effective image naming is crucial for SEO and accessibility:

- Be descriptive: Name images based on what they depict or their purpose. For instance, if it's an image of a cat, name it "cat.jpg" or "cute-cat.jpg" instead of generic names like "image1.jpg."
- Use keywords: Incorporate relevant keywords in image names to improve search engine optimization (SEO). For example, "red-rose.jpg" if the image is of a red rose.

- Use lowercase: Keep image file names in lowercase to ensure consistency.
- Include hyphens or underscores: Use hyphens or underscores to separate words in image file names.

Example:

- Good image name: "happy-family-at-the-beach.jpg"
- Bad image name: "IMG2023.jpg"

Consistency and clarity are key. Make sure your naming conventions are intuitive, and document them so others can follow the same system. This will help maintain a well-organized and user-friendly website or file system

4.7 Image Title and ALT Tags Creation :

Image title and ALT tags are elements of image metadata used in web development and content management to provide information about images on a website. They serve various purposes, including accessibility, search engine optimization (SEO), and user experience. Here's what each of these terms means:

1. Image Title:

- An image title is a descriptive text or label that you can assign to an image on a web page. It's typically used for improving user experience and can appear as a tooltip or a pop-up text when a user hovers their mouse pointer over the image.
- Image titles are not typically used for SEO but are helpful for providing additional context or information about the image, especially if the image is part of a gallery or contains important visual content.

2. ALT Tags (Alternative Text):

- ALT tags, short for "alternative text," are a critical component of web accessibility. They provide a text description of an image for individuals who are visually impaired or have difficulty viewing images. Screen readers, for example, rely on ALT tags to provide a spoken description of the image.
- ALT tags also play a significant role in SEO. Search engines use them to understand the content of images, which can contribute to the ranking of a web page in search results. When crafting ALT tags, it's important to use descriptive and relevant text that accurately conveys the image's content.

Creating Image Title and ALT Tags:

- To create an image title and ALT tag for an image on a website, you typically need to edit the HTML code of the web page where the image is displayed. Here's an example of how to do it:

  htmlCopy code

  ```
  <img src="example.jpg" alt="A red rose in full bloom" title="Beautiful Red Rose">
  ```

In the above example, "A red rose in full bloom" is the ALT tag, providing a description of the image for accessibility. "Beautiful Red Rose" is the image title, which could be used for user experience.

It's essential to make ALT tags descriptive and relevant to the image content while keeping image titles concise and informative. Properly utilizing these elements can enhance the accessibility, SEO, and overall user experience of your website.

Questions:

1. What is mean by Search Engine Optimization
2. Describe about Keyword Research with Google Keyword Planner.
3. Difference between Keyword Staffing & KW Placement
4. How to identify Selection of a Domain Name
5. Define page Naming (URL Structuring).
6. Compare between Keyword Stuffing & KW Placement.
7. Narrate about SEO Friendly Content Writing.
8. How webmaster tool is used in Search Engine Optimization.
9. Does the ALT tag serve as an alternative to the image content?
10. What information does a user need if the image doesn't load?

CHAPTER - V

5.1 Meaning of Meta Tags:

Meta tags are snippets of HTML code that provide information about a web page to search engines and website visitors. They are typically placed in the head section of an HTML document and are not visible on the web page itself. Meta tags serve several important functions, and different types of meta tags are used for various purposes. Here are some common types of meta tags and their meanings:

1. **Meta Title Tag (Title Element):**

- **Meaning:** The title tag defines the title of a web page and is displayed as the clickable link in search engine results pages (SERPs).
- **Example: <title>Your Page Title</title>**

2. **Meta Description Tag:**

- **Meaning:** The meta description tag provides a brief summary or description of the web page's content. It is often displayed below the title in search engine results.
- **Example: <meta name="description" content="A brief description of your page content">**

3. **Meta Keywords Tag (No longer widely used):**

- **Meaning:** In the past, this tag was used to list relevant keywords for a web page. However, most search engines no longer consider this tag when ranking pages, so it has become less important.
- **Example: <meta name = "keywords" content= "keyword1, keyword2, keyword3">**

4. **Meta Robots Tag:**

- **Meaning:** The meta robots tag instructs search engine crawlers on how to index and display a web page. It can be used to specify whether a page should be indexed, followed, or restricted from search results.
- **Example: <meta name="robots" content="index, follow">**

5. **Meta Viewport Tag:**

- **Meaning:** This tag is used for defining the viewport settings for responsive web design, which ensures that web pages display correctly on various devices and screen sizes.
- **Example: <meta name="viewport" content="width= device-width, initial-scale=1.0">**

6. **Other Meta Tags:**

- There are various other meta tags used for specific purposes, such as Open Graph meta tags for social media sharing, canonical tags to indicate the preferred version of a page, and more.

Meta tags are important for search engine optimization (SEO) as they help search engines understand the content and context of a web page. They also play a role in improving click-through rates in search results and enhancing the user experience. It's important to use meta tags effectively and ensure they accurately represent the content of your web pages.

5.2 Description meaning :

Description refers to a statement or representation that provides details or information about something, someone, or a particular situation. It is a way of conveying information in words, either in spoken or written form, to help others understand and visualize the subject being described. Descriptions can be used to clarify, explain, or paint a mental picture of a person, object, place, event, or concept.

In various contexts, the meaning of description can be more specific:

1. **Physical Description**: This involves providing details about the appearance of a person, object, or place. For example, describing someone's height, hair color, or the features of a landscape.
2. **Narrative Description**: In literature and storytelling, description is used to create vivid imagery and evoke sensory experiences. Authors use descriptive language to engage readers and make their writing more engaging.
3. **Product Description**: In marketing and e-commerce, a product description is a text that provides information about a product's features, benefits, and specifications to help potential customers make informed purchasing decisions.
4. **Job Description**: An outline of the duties, responsibilities, and qualifications required for a specific job position. Employers use job descriptions to communicate expectations to potential employees.
5. **Scientific Description**: In the sciences, description is essential for documenting and understanding natural phenomena. Scientists use detailed descriptions to record observations, experiments, and findings.
6. **Data Description**: In the context of data analysis, it involves summarizing and explaining the characteristics

and attributes of data sets. Data descriptions can include statistics, visualizations, and text explanations.

7. **Character Description**: In the context of character analysis in literature, it involves examining the personality, behavior, and development of fictional characters in a story.
8. **Geographical Description**: Providing information about the features, location, and characteristics of a geographic area, such as a city, country, or region.

Descriptions are valuable for communication and understanding, whether in everyday conversation, literature, marketing, science, or many other fields. They help convey information, create mental images, and facilitate effective communication.

5.3 Robots Meaning:

The term "robots" refers to machines or mechanical devices that can perform tasks autonomously or semi-autonomously, typically with the ability to carry out tasks programmatically and without direct human intervention. Robots can come in various forms and serve a wide range of functions, from industrial automation to household chores and even advanced applications like space exploration and medical procedures.

Key characteristics of robots include:

1. **Autonomy:** Robots can operate with varying degrees of autonomy, from being fully autonomous, capable of making decisions and taking actions without human input, to being teleoperated, where a human operator controls their movements and actions.

2. **Programmability:** Most robots are programmed to perform specific tasks or follow a set of instructions. This programming can be done through software or by manually configuring their hardware.
3. **Sensing and Perception:** Many robots are equipped with sensors and cameras to perceive their environment. These sensors enable them to gather data about their surroundings and make decisions based on that information.
4. **Mobility:** Robots can be stationary, like industrial robots in a factory, or mobile, like self-driving cars and drones. Mobility allows them to perform tasks in various locations.
5. **Manipulation:** Some robots are designed for physical interaction with objects and can manipulate them with arms, grippers, or other specialized tools.
6. **Versatility:** Robots can be specialized for a specific task, like welding or vacuuming, or they can be more versatile and adapt to different tasks through reprogramming or machine learning.
7. **Humanoid vs. Non-humanoid:** Robots come in a wide range of shapes and sizes. Some are designed to resemble humans (humanoid robots) for tasks that require human-like interaction, while others have unique, non-humanoid designs optimized for specific functions.

Robots have a long history and have evolved significantly in terms of their capabilities and applications. They play a crucial role in industries like manufacturing, healthcare, agriculture, and space exploration, as well as in everyday life. Advances in robotics continue to expand the possibilities for automation and the development of intelligent, autonomous machines.

Keywords:

Keywords are words or phrases that have special significance or importance in a particular context, such as in the context of search engines, programming, or academic research. The meaning of keywords can vary depending on the specific context, but generally, keywords are used to:

1. **Search Engines**: In the context of search engines like Google, keywords refer to the terms or phrases that users enter into the search bar to find relevant information on the internet. Search engines use these keywords to retrieve and display relevant web pages and other online content.
2. **Programming**: In computer programming, keywords are reserved words with predefined meanings in a programming language. They serve specific purposes and cannot be used as variable names or identifiers. For example, in the Python programming language, "if," "while," and "class" are keywords.
3. **Academic Research**: In the context of academic research and literature, keywords are specific terms or phrases that are used to describe the main concepts, topics, or themes of a document, such as a research paper, article, or book. Researchers use keywords to help others find their work in databases and libraries.
4. **Content Optimization**: In the realm of content creation, such as in digital marketing and SEO (Search Engine Optimization), keywords are the terms and phrases that are strategically included in web content to improve its visibility in search engine results. By targeting relevant keywords, website owners aim to attract more organic traffic.

The specific meaning of a keyword depends on the context in which it is used. Keywords are essential for effective communication, information retrieval, and content optimization in various fields

5.4 Author Redirection Tags headings Tags :

It seems like you're asking about different types of HTML tags and their purposes. Let's break down the terms you mentioned:

1. **Author Tags:** In the context of HTML, there's no specific tag referred to as "Author Tag." However, the authorship of a web page is typically indicated in the <meta> element using the "author" attribute. For example:
   htmlCopy code
   ```
   <meta name="author" content="John Doe">
   ```
   This is used to specify the author of the webpage.
2. **Redirection Tags:** Redirection typically involves automatically sending visitors from one URL to another. While this is often done through server-side techniques like using .htaccess files or server configurations, it can also be achieved using HTML meta refresh tags. For instance, to redirect users to another URL after a specified time, you can use the following code:
   htmlCopy code
   ```
   <meta http-equiv="refresh"
   content="5;url=http://example.com">
   ```
   This example will redirect the user to "http://example.com" after a 5-second delay.
3. **Headings Tags**: In HTML, headings are defined using <h1>, <h2>, <h3>, <h4>, <h5>, and <h6> tags. These tags are used to create hierarchical headings for your content. For example:

Html Copy code

<h1>This is a top-level heading</h1> <h2>This is a second-level heading</h2> <h3>This is a third-level heading</h3>

Headings help structure the content and make it more readable and accessible.

Please clarify if you have any specific questions or if you'd like more information on these HTML elements.

5.5 Meaning of Content Writing :

Content writing is the process of creating written material for online or offline platforms with the primary goal of conveying information, engaging an audience, or promoting a product, service, or idea. Content can take various forms, such as articles, blog posts, website copy, social media updates, product descriptions, press releases, and more.

The key objectives of content writing typically include:

1. **Informing:** Content should provide valuable and accurate information on a given topic to educate or inform the reader.
2. **Engaging:** Well-crafted content is designed to capture the reader's attention and maintain their interest throughout the piece.
3. **Persuading:** In marketing and advertising, content often aims to persuade the reader to take a specific action, such as making a purchase or signing up for a newsletter.
4. **SEO (Search Engine Optimization):** Content is frequently optimized to rank well in search engine results, making it more discoverable to online users. This involves using relevant keywords, quality writing, and other SEO techniques.

5. **Establishing authority:** High-quality content can help establish the author or the organization as an expert or authority in a particular field.
6. **Entertaining:** In the case of creative content, such as fiction, storytelling, or entertainment pieces, the primary goal may be to entertain or evoke emotions in the reader.

To be effective, content writing should be well-researched, well-structured, free of errors, and tailored to the target audience. It should also consider the medium or platform for which it is intended, as content for a blog will differ from content for a formal report, a social media post, or a product description. Content writers often need to be adaptable and versatile to create content that serves its intended purpose and reaches its target audience effectively.

5.6 SEO Friendly Content Writing :

Writing SEO-friendly content involves optimizing your web content to rank well in search engine results. One aspect of this optimization is to strategically insert relevant keywords into your content. Here are some guidelines on how to do it effectively:

1. **Keyword Research:** Start by conducting thorough keyword research to identify the keywords and phrases that your target audience is likely to use when searching for your content. Use tools like Google Keyword Planner, SEMrush, or Ahrefs to find relevant keywords.
2. **Understand User Intent:** It's not just about using keywords; you need to understand the user's intent behind those keywords. Are they looking for information, a product, or a service? Tailor your content to satisfy that intent.

3. **Quality Content:** Your content should always prioritize quality. Google's algorithms are getting smarter, and they reward high-quality, valuable content. Ensure your content is well-written, informative, and engaging.
4. **Keyword Placement:** Place your primary keyword in strategic locations within your content:
   - **Title:** Include the main keyword in your title if possible.
   - **Headers:** Use the keyword in subheadings (H2, H3 tags) where appropriate.
   - **First Paragraph:** Incorporate the keyword naturally in the opening paragraph.
   - **Throughout the Content:** Sprinkle the keyword naturally throughout the content, but don't overdo it. Aim for a keyword density of around 1-2%.
   - **Meta Description:** Include the keyword in your meta description.
5. **Use Synonyms and Related Terms:** Rather than overusing the exact keyword, incorporate synonyms and related terms. This helps your content appear more natural and can capture a broader range of search queries.
6. **Long-Tail Keywords:** Don't just focus on broad keywords. Long-tail keywords (more specific, longer phrases) can be less competitive and attract a highly targeted audience.
7. **User Experience:** Ensure your content is easily readable and scannable. Use bullet points, short paragraphs, and headings to break up the text.
8. **Mobile Optimization:** Make sure your content is mobile-friendly as Google prioritizes mobile-first indexing.
9. **Avoid Keyword Stuffing:** Keyword stuffing (repeatedly using the same keyword unnaturally) can harm your SEO.

Google may penalize or de-rank your content for this practice.

10. **Regularly Update Content:** Keep your content fresh and up to date. Search engines favor recently updated content.
11. **Internal and External Links:** Include relevant internal links to other pages on your website and high-quality external links to authoritative sources.
12. **Image Optimization:** Use descriptive file names and alt tags for images, and compress them to improve page loading speed.
13. **Meta Tags:** Optimize your meta title and meta description with relevant keywords and a call to action.

Remember that SEO is an ongoing process, and it may take time to see significant results. Focus on providing value to your audience and keep up with the latest SEO best practices as search engine algorithms evolve.

Questions: 5

1. What are meta tags, and how do they play a crucial role in website development?
2. Could you explain the primary purpose of using meta tags in HTML documents?
3. How do meta tags contribute to search engine optimization (SEO)?
4. Can you elaborate on how search engines use meta tags to index and rank web pages?
5. How do author redirection tags impact search engine optimization?
6. What are the common types of author redirection tags, and how are they implemented?

7. Can author redirection tags be used to consolidate content from multiple URLs?
8. How does this content differentiate itself from similar content already available?
9. What is the main focus keyword for the content?
10. Does the content have a clear structure with headings and subheadings?

CHAPTER - VI

6.1 Anchor Text Meaning:

Anchor text is the visible, clickable text in a hyperlink. It is the text that is typically highlighted or underlined and is used to provide a concise description of the linked web page's content or the destination of the link. Anchor text is significant for both users and search engines because it gives users an idea of what to expect when they click on the link and helps search engines understand the context and relevance of the linked page.

For example, in the HTML code <a href = "https://www.example.com"> Click here to visit Example.com</a>, "Click here to visit Example.com" is the anchor text. When users click on this link, they are taken to the website "https://www.example.com."

Effective use of anchor text is essential for search engine optimization (SEO) because search engines use anchor text as a signal to determine the topic or theme f the linked page. Properly optimized anchor text can contribute to higher search engine rankings and better user experience. It's important to use descriptive and relevant anchor text that accurately reflects the content of the linked page. Overuse of keyword-rich anchor text or overly optimized anchor text can be seen as spammy by search engines and may result in penalties.

6.2 Link Title Internal Linking Robot :

Internal linking refers to the practice of linking to other pages within the same website or domain, and "robots" might refer to search engine bots that crawl and index web pages.

6.3 Text File use and Creation HTML :

A text file is a file that contains only plain text characters and no special formatting, styles, or binary data. Text files are used for storing and representing textual information and can be created and read using various programming languages, text editors, and software applications. HTML, which stands for Hypertext Markup Language, is a markup language commonly used to create web pages and format text content for the World Wide Web.

Here's a brief overview of the use and creation of text files and HTML:

Text File:

1. **Use:**

- Text files are used for storing and exchanging plain text information. They can contain various types of data, such as program source code, configuration settings, documentation, or simple text-based data like CSV (Comma-Separated Values) files.
- Text files are often used for data interchange and storage because they are human-readable and can be processed by many different software applications.

2. **Creation:**

- Text files can be created using text editors, code editors, or programming languages.

- In most text editors and code editors, you can create a new text file and start typing or pasting text.
- In programming languages like Python, you can create and write to a text file using functions like open() and write().
- Text files typically have file extensions like .txt, .csv, or .log.

HTML (Hypertext Markup Language):

1. **Use:**

- HTML is used to create the structure and content of web pages. It defines the elements and their layout on a web page, allowing you to display text, images, links, and other media.
- HTML is the foundation of web development and is often used in conjunction with CSS (Cascading Style Sheets) and JavaScript to create interactive and visually appealing websites.

2. **Creation:**

- HTML documents are created using plain text editors, code editors, or integrated development environments (IDEs).
- An HTML document starts with an HTML tag (<html>) and typically includes elements like headings (<h1>, <h2>), paragraphs (<p>), links (<a>), images (<img>), and many others.
- You save HTML files with the .html file extension.
- Once created, HTML documents can be viewed in web browsers to render the content as a web page.

Here's a simple example of an HTML document:

```
<!DOCTYPE html>
<html>
<head>
    <title>My Web Page</title>
</head>
<body>
    <h1>Welcome to My Web Page</h1>
    <p>This is a sample web page created with HTML.</p>
    <a href="https://www.example.com">Visit
    Example.com</a>
</body>
</html>
```

This HTML document defines the structure and content of a basic web page. When opened in a web browser, it displays the title, heading, paragraph, and a hyperlink to Example.com.

6.4 Sitemap Creation:

A sitemap creation is the process of generating a file or web page that lists and provides information about the pages, posts, and other content on a website. This file or page is called a sitemap, and it serves several important purposes, primarily for search engines and website visitors. Here are the key aspects of sitemap creation:

1. **Search Engine Optimization (SEO):** Sitemaps help search engines like Google, Bing, and others to better understand the structure of a website and the relationships between its various pages. This makes it easier for search engines to index the content, resulting in better search engine rankings.

2. **Crawling Efficiency:** Search engine crawlers, also known as bots or spiders, use sitemaps to navigate and index a website more efficiently. Instead of having to discover all pages through links on a site, they can simply follow the links in the sitemap.
3. **Content Organization:** Sitemaps can be used to organize a website's content logically, indicating which pages are more important or which are part of specific categories or sections. This helps both search engines and users find relevant content easily.
4. **User Experience:** Some websites provide HTML sitemaps that are intended for human users, allowing them to quickly find and navigate to specific pages on the site. This can enhance the user experience, especially on larger websites.
5. **XML vs. HTML Sitemaps:** There are two primary types of sitemaps:
   - **XML Sitemaps:** These are created specifically for search engines. They are typically not seen by users and are formatted in a way that is easy for search engine crawlers to read. XML sitemaps often include additional information such as when each page was last updated.
   - **HTML Sitemaps:** These are designed for human users and are often structured as a web page with clickable links to various pages on the site.

Sitemap creation can be done manually, with the webmaster or website administrator crafting the sitemap, or it can be automated using tools and plugins, which are commonly available for popular website content management systems like Word Press. Search engines encourage website owners to submit their XML sitemaps through their webmaster tools to aid in the indexing process.

In summary, sitemap creation is a fundamental part of website management, assisting in SEO, efficient crawling, content organization, and improved user experience.

6.5 XML Site Map Creation Site Tracking Tools :

ML Sitemap Creation and Site Tracking Tools:

1. **XML Sitemap Creation:**

- **XML Sitemap**: An XML sitemap is a file that lists all the URLs of a website, helping search engines like Google and Bing understand the site's structure and content. It's an essential tool for search engine optimization (SEO). Here's how you can create an XML sitemap:
- **Manual Creation**: You can create an XML sitemap manually using a text editor, but it's typically more efficient to use automated tools or plugins.
- **Automated Tools/Plugins**: Many website platforms, content management systems, and SEO tools offer plugins or built-in features for generating XML sitemaps. Some popular tools include Yoast SEO (for WordPress), Screaming Frog, and Google Search Console (for submitting sitemaps).

6.6 Site Tracking Tools:

Site Tracking: Site tracking tools are used to monitor and analyze the performance and user interactions on a website. They provide valuable data that helps website owners and marketers make informed decisions. Some common features and tools for site tracking include:

- **Google Analytics**: A widely-used free tool that tracks website traffic, user behavior, and conversion rates. It provides detailed reports on user demographics, source of traffic, and more.
- **Google Search Console**: Offers insights into how Googlebot views your site and helps identify and fix technical issues affecting search engine visibility.
- **Hotjar**: Provides heatmaps, session recordings, and user surveys to understand how visitors interact with your site.
- **Adobe Analytics**: A comprehensive analytics solution that tracks user behavior, supports A/B testing, and offers deep insights into customer journeys.
- **Mouseflow**: Offers session replay, heatmaps, and conversion funnel analysis to track user behavior.
- **Kissmetrics**: Focuses on customer engagement and provides insights into user journeys, customer segmentation, and more.
- **Matomo**: An open-source web analytics platform that can be self-hosted, giving you control over your data.
- **Segment**: A customer data platform that collects, cleans, and sends data to various analytics tools and marketing platforms.

In summary, creating an XML sitemap is essential for SEO, and there are various tools and plugins available to automate this process. Site tracking tools help you gather data about user behavior and website performance, enabling you to optimize your site for better user experiences and business outcomes.

Webmaster Tool Introduction:

Webmaster tools, often referred to as Search Console or Site Tools, are a set of online tools provided by major search engines like Google and Bing. These tools are designed to help webmasters, website owners, and SEO professionals monitor, analyze, and optimize the performance of their websites in search engine results. Here's a general introduction to webmaster tools:

1. **Google Search Console**:

- Google Search Console is a free tool provided by Google. It's one of the most widely used webmaster tools, and it offers various features to help you understand how your website is performing in Google search.
- Key features include the ability to submit your sitemap, monitor indexing status, check for crawl errors, view search analytics data, and receive alerts regarding issues with your site.

2. **Bing Webmaster Tools**:

- Bing offers a similar suite of tools for webmasters. It allows you to submit your site to the Bing search engine, monitor its performance, and resolve issues that might affect how your site appears in Bing search results.

3. **Yandex Webmaster**:

- Yandex, a popular search engine in Russia, offers webmaster tools to help site owners understand how their sites perform in Yandex search results. It provides data on indexing, traffic, and more.

4. **Yahoo Site Explorer (now integrated with Bing)**:

- Yahoo Site Explorer was a popular tool for Yahoo search, but after the Microsoft-Yahoo partnership, it's now integrated with Bing Webmaster Tools.

Key Functions of Webmaster Tools:

- **Sitemap Submission**: You can submit a sitemap of your website to help search engines better understand its structure and content.
- **Crawl Control**: These tools allow you to control how search engines crawl and index your site, such as setting crawl rates or blocking specific pages.
- **Indexing Status**: You can check which pages of your website are indexed by search engines and which ones might be excluded.
- **Search Performance Data**: View data on how your website is performing in search results, including clicks, impressions, and average positions.
- **Mobile-Friendly Testing**: Ensure that your site is mobile-friendly and get recommendations for improvements.

Webmaster tools are essential for optimizing your website's visibility in search engine results, improving user experience, and ensuring that your site is in compliance with search engine guidelines. Regularly monitoring these tools and taking action based on the data they provide can help enhance your website's performance and overall online presence.

Google Analytics:

Google Analytics is a web analytics service provided by Google that allows website and app owners to track and analyze various aspects of user interaction with their online properties. It provides valuable insights into how users engage with a website, mobile app, or other digital platforms, helping businesses and website operators make data-driven decisions to improve user experiences and achieve their objectives.

Key features and capabilities of Google Analytics include:

1. **Traffic Analysis:** It tracks the source of website or app traffic, including the channels (e.g., organic search, paid advertising, direct, social media) and geographic location of visitors.
2. **User Behavior:** Google Analytics provides data on how users navigate through a website, including pageviews, session duration, bounce rate, and conversion events.
3. **Audience Insights**: It offers demographic and interest-based information about website visitors, helping businesses better understand their audience.
4. **E-commerce Tracking:** For online stores, it can track e-commerce-related metrics such as revenue, transactions, and product performance.
5. **Conversion Tracking:** Users can define and track specific goals and conversions, such as form submissions, downloads, or purchases.
6. **Event Tracking:** This feature allows you to monitor user interactions with specific elements on a page, like video plays or button clicks.
7. **Custom Reports and Dashboards**: Google Analytics enables users to create customized reports and dashboards to focus on the data most relevant to their goals.
8. **Real-Time Monitoring:** You can see what is happening on your website in real time, including active users, traffic sources, and the content they are viewing.

9. **Integration with Other Google Services:** Google Analytics can be integrated with other Google products, like Google Ads and Google Search Console, to provide a more comprehensive view of online marketing efforts.

To use Google Analytics, website or app owners need to install a tracking code (usually JavaScript) on their site, which collects and sends data to Google's servers. The collected data is then presented in the Google Analytics interface, where users can generate reports, analyze trends, and gain insights into how their digital properties are performing.

Google Analytics offers both free and paid versions. The paid version, called Google Analytics 360 (now known as Google Analytics for Firebase and Google Analytics for Google Marketing Platform), is designed for enterprises with more extensive data tracking and analysis needs.

6.7 Alexa:

Alexa is a virtual assistant AI (artificial intelligence) developed by Amazon. It is primarily known for its integration into Amazon's Echo and Echo Dot smart speakers and other devices. Alexa is designed to respond to voice commands and perform various tasks and services for users. These tasks can include answering questions, setting alarms, providing weather forecasts, playing music, controlling smart home devices, and more. Alexa uses natural language processing and machine learning to understand and interpret user commands and queries, making it a versatile and user-friendly voice-activated assistant. It can also be extended through third-party skills and apps, allowing developers to create additional functionalities for Alexa.

6.8 Alexa Integration:

Alexa integration refers to the process of incorporating Amazon's virtual assistant, Alexa, into various devices or applications to enable voice-controlled interactions and access to the wide range of services and skills offered by Alexa. This integration allows users to use voice commands to interact with devices or access information, perform tasks, control smart home devices, and more.

There are several ways to integrate Alexa into various platforms:

1. **Alexa-enabled devices:** These are physical devices like Amazon Echo smart speakers, Echo Show, or Echo Dot that come with Alexa built-in. Users can interact with these devices by using voice commands to play music, set alarms, control smart home devices, and more.
2. **Alexa Skills:** Developers can create third-party applications, known as "skills," that expand Alexa's functionality. Users can enable these skills to perform specific tasks or access particular services. For example, you can enable a news skill to get updates, a weather skill to check the weather forecast, or a smart home skill to control compatible devices.
3. **Alexa Voice Service (AVS):** AVS allows manufacturers to integrate Alexa into their own hardware devices, such as smart TVs, cars, and appliances. This brings voice-controlled functionality to a wide range of products beyond Amazon's own devices.
4. **Alexa for Business:** This integration is tailored for the workplace, enabling businesses to use Alexa to schedule meetings, control office equipment, or access corporate data.

5. **Alexa Skills Kit (ASK):** Developers can use ASK to build custom Alexa skills that can be used in a wide range of applications, from entertainment and gaming to productivity and education.

Overall, Alexa integration enhances the user experience by making it more convenient to interact with technology and access information and services through voice commands. It has gained popularity in smart homes, automotive systems, and various other applications.

Questions : 6

1. Describe about Alexa and Alexa Integration.
2. Write about the Meaning of Content Writing and explain Briefly.
3. Explain about Site Map Creation and Site Map tool
4. What specific actions or tasks do you want users to perform using Alexa?
5. Are you planning to use Alexa for simple commands, or do you want to implement more complex interactions?
6. What existing systems or services will Alexa need to integrate with?
7. Are there any APIs or third-party services you plan to connect with via Alexa?
8. Explain about Image Title and ALT Tags Creation?
9. Difference about folder naming and Image Naming?
10. Discuss about Selection of a Domain Name ?

CHAPTER - VII

7.1 Off Page SEO Introduction:

Off-page SEO refers to the various techniques and strategies used to improve the visibility and reputation of a website or webpage on search engine results pages (SERPs) and across the broader online landscape. Unlike on-page SEO, which focuses on optimizing the content and structure of a website, off-page SEO is concerned with factors that occur off the website itself. Off-page SEO is essential for building trust, authority, and credibility with search engines and users alike.

Off-page SEO (Search Engine Optimization) refers to the activities and strategies that you implement outside of your website to improve its visibility and ranking in search engine results pages (SERPs). It involves optimizing various factors that are not directly controlled on your website but can have a significant impact on your site's authority, trustworthiness, and relevance in the eyes of search engines like Google. Off-page SEO primarily focuses on building a strong online presence and reputation to boost your website's rankings.

7.2 Meaning:

Off-page SEO refers to the various activities and strategies that are undertaken outside of your own website to improve its search engine rankings and overall online visibility. It is an essential component of search engine optimization (SEO), alongside on-page SEO, which focuses on optimizing elements within your website.

Off-page SEO primarily revolves around building your website's reputation and authority in the eyes of search engines, particularly Google. The main goal is to signal to search engines that your website is credible, trustworthy, and relevant to users.

Elements of Off page SEO:

Link Building: One of the most crucial aspects of off-page SEO is acquiring high-quality backlinks from other reputable websites. These backlinks serve as "votes of confidence" from other sites, indicating that your content is valuable and trustworthy. Quality is more important than quantity, so focus on getting links from authoritative, relevant sources.

- **Social Media Marketing:** Active participation on social media platforms can help you promote your content, engage with your audience, and increase your website's visibility. Social signals (likes, shares, comments) can indirectly influence search engine rankings.
- **Content Marketing:** Creating and promoting high-quality, shareable content like blog posts, infographics, videos, and ebooks can attract natural backlinks and increase your website's authority. Guest posting on authoritative websites in your industry is another way to gain exposure and build links.
- **Online Reputation Management:** Monitoring and managing your online reputation is essential. Positive reviews and mentions can enhance your website's credibility, while negative ones can harm it. Encourage happy customers to leave reviews and address any negative feedback promptly.

- **Local SEO:** If you have a physical location or serve a specific geographic area, optimizing for local search is critical. This involves creating and maintaining a Google My Business listing, obtaining local citations, and garnering positive reviews from local customers.
- **Influencer Outreach:** Partnering with influencers in your niche can help you reach a broader audience and build authority in your industry. Influencers can promote your content or products to their followers, potentially driving traffic and backlinks.
- **Social Bookmarking:** Sharing your content on social bookmarking sites like Reddit, StumbleUpon, or Digg can help expose your content to a wider audience. However, be cautious not to spam these platforms, as this can have a negative impact.
- **Forum Participation:** Engaging in forums and discussion boards relevant to your niche can establish you as an authority in your field. Include a link to your website in your forum signature when appropriate, but always provide valuable contributions to the community.
- **Brand Mentions:** Even when there are no direct links to your website, brand mentions across the web can contribute to your online presence. Monitoring mentions and engaging with them can be beneficial.
- **Press Releases:** Distributing well-crafted press releases about significant events or news related to your business can help you gain exposure and potentially earn links from news outlets and industry-specific websites.

Off-page SEO is an ongoing process that requires time, effort, and a well-thought-out strategy. It complements on-page SEO (optimizing elements on your website itself) and is crucial for improving your website's search engine rankings and overall online visibility. Keep in mind that search engines continually update their algorithms, so staying up-to-date with best practices in off-page SEO is essential for long-term success

Key Components of Off Page SEO:

- **Backlinks:** Backlinks are links from other websites that point to your site. High-quality and relevant backlinks from authoritative websites are crucial for search engine rankings. Search engines view these backlinks as votes of confidence in your content.
- **Social Media:** Engaging with social media platforms and promoting your content through them can help increase your online presence. Social signals, such as likes, shares, and comments, can indirectly impact your SEO by driving traffic and demonstrating popularity.
- **Content Marketing:** Creating high-quality, shareable content that attracts natural backlinks is a core off-page SEO strategy. This can include blog posts, infographics, videos, and more.
- **Guest Blogging:** Writing and publishing articles on other authoritative websites within your niche can help you gain exposure, build relationships, and earn backlinks to your site.
- **Online Reputation Management:** Managing your online reputation is crucial. Monitoring and responding to online reviews, comments, and mentions can positively impact how your brand is perceived and affect your search engine rankings.

- **Local SEO:** For businesses with a physical presence, optimizing for local search is essential. This includes creating and optimizing your Google My Business listing, acquiring local citations, and getting reviews from satisfied customers.
- **Influencer Outreach:** Collaborating with influencers in your industry can help you reach a wider audience and gain credibility within your niche.
- **Social Bookmarking:** Sharing your website's content on social bookmarking sites like Reddit, Digg, and StumbleUpon can drive traffic and increase your content's visibility.
- **Forum Participation:** Engaging in relevant online forums and communities allows you to establish your expertise, answer questions, and include links to your site when relevant.
- **Link Building Strategies:** Developing a diverse and natural link profile is essential. Avoid black-hat techniques like buying links or engaging in link schemes, as they can lead to penalties from search engines.

It's important to note that off-page SEO is an ongoing process that requires time and effort. Building a strong online presence and earning high-quality backlinks can take months or even years, but the long-term benefits in terms of improved search rankings and organic traffic are well worth the investment. Additionally, staying up-to-date with search engine algorithms and industry trends is crucial for a successful off-page SEO strategy.

Meaning of Off Page Optimization:

Off-page optimization, also known as off-site optimization, is a crucial aspect of search engine optimization (SEO). It refers to the various activities and strategies that are implemented outside of your website to improve its visibility and authority in search engine results pages (SERPs). Off-page optimization aims to enhance your website's reputation, credibility, and relevance in the eyes of search engines and users.

Key components of off-page optimization include:

- **Backlink Building:** One of the most important off-page SEO techniques is building high-quality backlinks from other reputable websites to your own. Backlinks serve as votes of confidence in your content and can significantly impact your website's rankings. It's essential to acquire natural and relevant backlinks rather than resorting to spammy or unethical practices.
- **Social Media Engagement:** Engaging with your audience on social media platforms can help increase your website's visibility and drive traffic. Sharing content, interacting with followers, and building a strong social media presence can indirectly benefit your SEO efforts.
- **Content Marketing:** Creating high-quality, shareable content is a fundamental aspect of off-page optimization. When your content is valuable and relevant, other websites and users are more likely to link to it, share it on social media, or reference it in their own content.
- **Influencer Outreach:** Collaborating with influencers in your niche can help you reach a broader audience and gain valuable backlinks and mentions. Influencers can

promote your content or products to their followers, boosting your website's authority and credibility.

- **Online Reputation Management:** Monitoring and managing your online reputation is crucial. Responding to customer reviews, addressing negative feedback, and maintaining a positive online image can indirectly affect your search engine rankings.
- **Local SEO:** If your business has a physical location, optimizing for local search is essential. This involves creating and optimizing local business listings, collecting positive reviews, and ensuring accurate and consistent NAP (Name, Address, Phone number) information across the web.
- **Guest Posting:** Contributing guest posts to reputable websites in your industry can help you build authority and gain backlinks. However, it's important to do this in a way that provides genuine value and follows ethical guidelines.
- **Brand Mentions:** When other websites or social media users mention your brand or website without linking to it, it can still be beneficial for your SEO. These brand mentions contribute to your online reputation and can indirectly influence your search engine rankings.
- Off-page optimization complements on-page optimization, which involves optimizing elements within your website, such as content, meta tags, and site structure. Both on-page and off-page SEO are essential for achieving higher search engine rankings and driving organic traffic to your website.

7.3 Backlinks:

Backlinks, also known as inbound links or incoming links, are hyperlinks on one website that point to another website. These links are crucial in the field of search engine optimization (SEO) and play a significant role in determining a website's search engine ranking. Here's some important information about backlinks:

- **Purpose**: Backlinks serve several purposes, including directing traffic from one website to another and improving a website's authority and credibility in the eyes of search engines.
- **SEO Importance**: Search engines like Google consider backlinks as a vote of confidence from one site to another. The more high-quality and relevant backlinks a website has, the more likely it is to rank higher in search engine results pages (SERPs).
- **Types of Backlinks**:
  1. **Natural Backlinks**: These are links that other websites create voluntarily because they find the content valuable or relevant.
  2. **Manual Backlinks**: These are links that website owners actively build by reaching out to other websites, submitting to directories, or participating in link-building strategies.
  3. **Editorial Backlinks**: When a website links to another because it genuinely believes the linked content is useful, it's considered an editorial backlink. These are highly valuable.
  4. **Guest Post Backlinks**: Websites often allow guest bloggers to contribute content in exchange for a

backlink to their site. This is a common link-building strategy.

5. **Nofollow and Dofollow Links**: Nofollow links tell search engines not to pass authority to the linked page, while dofollow links do. Both types can be valuable for SEO, depending on the context.

- **Quality Over Quantity**: It's important to focus on the quality of backlinks rather than the sheer number. High-quality backlinks from authoritative and relevant websites carry more weight in SEO.
- **Anchor Text**: The text used in the hyperlink (anchor text) is essential. It should be relevant to the linked page's content and should include keywords you want to rank for.
- **Link Building Strategies**: To acquire backlinks, website owners often engage in various link-building strategies, such as guest posting, broken link building, outreach to bloggers and influencers, and creating high-quality, shareable content.
- **Avoiding Spammy Practices**: Building backlinks through spammy tactics like buying links or participating in link farms can harm your website's SEO and reputation. It's essential to focus on ethical and organic link-building methods.
- **Monitoring and Disavowing**: Website owners should regularly monitor their backlink profiles to identify any low-quality or harmful links. If necessary, they can use Google's Disavow Tool to ask the search engine not to consider specific links.
- **Evolving SEO Landscape**: Search engine algorithms are constantly evolving, and the importance of various

ranking factors, including backlinks, may change over time. Staying updated on SEO best practices is crucial.

- In summary, backlinks are a vital element of SEO and can significantly impact a website's search engine ranking and online visibility. However, it's essential to focus on acquiring high-quality, relevant backlinks through ethical practices to achieve the best results.

7.4 Importance of backlinks:

Backlinks, also known as inbound links or incoming links, are links from one website to another. They play a crucial role in the field of search engine optimization (SEO) and are important for several reasons:

- **Improved Search Engine Rankings**: Backlinks are a fundamental factor in how search engines like Google rank web pages. Search engines consider backlinks as a vote of confidence or trust from one site to another. Websites with a higher number of quality backlinks tend to rank higher in search results for relevant keywords.
- **Increased Organic Traffic**: When your website has high-quality backlinks from authoritative sources, it is more likely to appear in search results for relevant queries. This can lead to an increase in organic (non-paid) traffic to your site, as users are more likely to click on links that appear near the top of search results.
- **Credibility and Trust**: Backlinks from reputable and trustworthy websites can lend credibility and authority to your own site. When a reputable website links to yours, it signals to users and search engines that your content is valuable and trustworthy.

- **Referral Traffic**: Backlinks can also generate direct referral traffic to your website. If a user on another site clicks on a link leading to your site, they are referred to your site, potentially increasing your audience and customer base.
- **Content Promotion**: Backlinks can be a way to promote your content to a wider audience. When other websites link to your blog posts, articles, or other valuable content, it exposes your content to their audience, increasing its visibility.
- **Relationship Building**: Building backlinks often involves outreach to other website owners or bloggers. This outreach can lead to relationship-building opportunities, collaborations, and partnerships in your industry or niche.
- **Diversification of Traffic Sources**: Relying solely on one traffic source, such as social media or paid advertising, can be risky. Backlinks provide another avenue for attracting traffic to your website, reducing your dependence on a single source.

However, it's important to note that not all backlinks are equal. Quality matters more than quantity. High-quality backlinks come from reputable and authoritative websites that are relevant to your content. Low-quality or spammy backlinks can actually harm your SEO efforts and may result in penalties from search engines.

To build a strong backlink profile, it's essential to focus on creating valuable, shareable content, fostering relationships with other website owners and bloggers in your niche, and following ethical and SEO best practices. Additionally, keep in mind that SEO is a long-term strategy, and the impact of backlinks may take time to be fully realized.

7.5 Getting Backlinks:

Getting backlinks, also known as inbound links or incoming links, is an important aspect of search engine optimization (SEO). Backlinks are links from other websites that point to your website. They are valuable because search engines like Google consider them as a vote of confidence in your site's content and authority. Here are some legitimate ways to acquire backlinks:

- **Create High-Quality Content**: The most effective way to attract backlinks is to create high-quality, informative, and engaging content that others find valuable. When your content is exceptional, other websites are more likely to link to it as a reference.
- **Guest Blogging**: Write guest posts for other reputable websites in your niche. Include a link back to your website within the article or in your author bio. Ensure that the content is relevant and valuable to the host site's audience.
- **Link Outreach:** Reach out to other website owners, bloggers, and influencers in your industry. Politely ask if they would be interested in linking to your content if it's relevant to their audience. Personalize your outreach messages and make it clear how their audience will benefit from the link.
- **Broken Link Building**: Identify broken links on other websites in your niche, and offer your content as a replacement. This technique can provide a win-win situation for both parties.
- **Social Media Sharing**: Promote your content on social media platforms to increase its visibility. When others see and appreciate your content, they may naturally link to it from their websites and social profiles.

- **Directories and Resource Pages**: Submit your website to relevant online directories, industry-specific resource pages, and local business listings. Ensure that these directories are reputable and relevant to your niche.
- **Collaborate on Projects:** Collaborate with other content creators or businesses on projects, such as ebooks, webinars, or research studies. This can lead to backlinks when partners link to the collaborative content on their websites.
- **Press Releases**: Write and distribute press releases about noteworthy events or developments related to your business. Many online press release distribution services allow you to include links.
- **Community Engagement**: Participate in online communities, forums, and discussion boards related to your niche. Be helpful and share your expertise. Some forums allow you to include a link in your forum signature or user profile.
- **Create Infographics and Visual Content**: Infographics and visual content are highly shareable. If you create visually appealing and informative graphics, other websites may link to them as a resource.

Remember that quality matters more than quantity when it comes to backlinks. Focus on acquiring backlinks from reputable and authoritative websites in your niche. Avoid tactics like buying backlinks or engaging in link schemes, as these can lead to penalties from search engines and harm your website's SEO.

Additionally, SEO is an ongoing process, and it takes time to build a strong backlink profile. Be patient and continue to produce valuable content and engage with your industry's community to naturally attract backlinks over time.

7.6 Do-Follow& No-Follow:

Do-Follow Meaning

In the context of SEO (Search Engine Optimization) and link-building, "do-follow" refers to a type of hyperlink attribute that tells search engines to follow and pass authority or "link juice" from one webpage to another. When a website or webpage has a "do-follow" link pointing to another website, it means that search engines like Google should consider that link as a signal for ranking purposes.

Here's a bit more detail:

- Do-Follow Links: These are regular hyperlinks that are not explicitly marked with a "nofollow" attribute in the HTML code. When a search engine crawler encounters a do-follow link, it will follow that link to the linked page and consider it when determining the linked page's ranking and authority. These links can contribute to improving a website's SEO because they pass on some of the SEO "juice" to the linked page.
- Nofollow Links: In contrast, "nofollow" links are hyperlinks that have the "nofollow" attribute in their HTML code. This attribute tells search engines not to follow the link or pass any SEO authority to the linked page. Nofollow links are often used for user-generated content, comments, or links where the website owner does not want to vouch for the credibility of the linked content.

So, when you hear the term "do-follow," it generally means a link that is valuable for SEO purposes because it can positively influence the linked page's search engine rankings. However, it's essential to use do-follow links judiciously and within the guidelines provided by search engines to avoid penalties for unnatural link building

No-Follow Meaning:

A "no-follow" link or attribute is a designation used in HTML to tell search engines not to follow or crawl a particular hyperlink. When a link is marked as "no-follow," it signals to search engine crawlers that they should not pass any link equity or "link juice" from the linking page to the linked page. In other words, it tells search engines not to consider the linked page as an endorsement or recommendation by the linking page.

The primary purpose of using the "no-follow" attribute is to control the flow of PageRank (a metric used by Google to determine the importance of web pages) and prevent search engines from counting certain links when determining a page's ranking in search results. This is often done to prevent spammy or low-quality links from influencing a website's search engine ranking.

The syntax for adding a "no-follow" attribute to a link in HTML looks like this:

```
<a href="https://example.com" rel="nofollow">Link
Text</a>
```

By including "rel="nofollow"" in the anchor tag, you indicate to search engines that this link should not be followed or used to influence search rankings. It's commonly used in user-generated content like blog comments and forum posts to discourage spammy link-building practices.

Difference Between Do-Follow & No-Follow:-

Dofollow and nofollow are two different types of HTML attributes used in hyperlinks on websites. These attributes dictate how search engines like Google should treat the links for the purpose of search engine optimization (SEO) and ranking.

- **Dofollow Backlinks**:
  1. Dofollow backlinks are regular hyperlinks that do not contain the "nofollow" attribute in their HTML code.
  2. When a website links to another site using a dofollow link, it passes link equity or "link juice" to the linked site.
  3. Search engines like Google consider dofollow links as votes of confidence from one site to another. They use these links to assess the authority and credibility of the linked page.
  4. Dofollow links can positively impact the search engine rankings of the linked page if they come from reputable and authoritative sources.

- **No follow Back links**:

1. No follow back links, on the other hand, include the "no follow" attribute in their HTML code. This attribute tells search engines not to follow the link and not to pass any link equity or Page Rank to the linked page.

2. No follow links are often used for user-generated content, paid links, or links where the website owner doesn't want to vouch for the credibility of the linked content.
3. While nofollow links don't directly influence search engine rankings, they can still drive traffic to the linked page if users click on them. Additionally, they can be valuable for diversifying a website's back link profile.

In summary, the key difference between do follow and no follow back links is whether they pass link equity or not. Do-follow links are seen as endorsements and can impact search engine rankings positively, while no-follow links are used for various purposes but do not directly influence SEO rankings. Both types of links have their place in a well-rounded SEO strategy, and a natural back link profile typically includes a mix of both.

7.7 Meaning of Google Page Rank:

Google Page Rank, often simply referred to as Page Rank, is an algorithm developed by Larry Page and Sergey Brin, the co-founders of Google, while they were graduate students at Stanford University. It was one of the fundamental components of Google's search engine when it was first introduced in the late 1990s. Page Rank is named after Larry Page.

The basic idea behind Page Rank is to assess the importance of web pages on the World Wide Web based on their link structure. In other words, it aims to determine the significance or authority of a webpage by analyzing the number and quality of links pointing to it from other web pages. The underlying assumption is that valuable and relevant content tends to attract more links from other web pages.

Here's how Page Rank works in a simplified manner:

- Each webpage is treated as a node in a network graph.
- Links between web pages are represented as edges in this graph.
- Page Rank is calculated iteratively, assigning an initial Page Rank value to each page.
- In each iteration, the Page Rank value of a page is updated based on the Page Rank values of the pages linking to it.
- The more inbound links (back links) a page has from reputable and authoritative sources, the more influential its Page Rank becomes.
- Page Rank values are redistributed in each iteration until they converge to a stable set of values. This process helps identify which web pages are considered more important or authoritative in the network.
- Pages with higher Page Rank are generally considered to be more valuable or relevant in the context of search results.

It's important to note that while Page Rank played a significant role in Google's early search algorithm, it is no longer the sole or even the primary factor in determining search engine rankings. Google has since developed more complex algorithms that take into account numerous other factors, including content relevance, user engagement, and user experience.

Page Rank is also just one part of Google's overall ranking algorithm, and it's been updated and refined over the years. Additionally, Google doesn't publicly disclose the specifics of how PageRank is calculated or the weight it carries in its current ranking algorithm. Nevertheless, the concept of assessing a webpage's importance based on its links remains a fundamental aspect of search engine optimization (SEO) strategies

Importance of Google Page Rank:

Google PageRank was once a crucial component of Google's search algorithm, but its importance has diminished significantly over the years. However, understanding its historical significance can provide insight into the evolution of search engine technology and the ongoing importance of certain principles in the field of SEO (Search Engine Optimization). Here are some key points highlighting the importance of Google Page Rank:

- **Pioneering Algorithm**: Google Page Rank was one of the first algorithms developed by Google's co-founders, Larry Page and Sergey Brin. It played a pivotal role in Google's early success by providing a more sophisticated and effective way to rank web pages compared to other search engines at the time.
- **Link Analysis**: Page Rank introduced the concept of link analysis, which assessed the importance of a web page based on the number and quality of links pointing to it. This concept laid the foundation for modern search engine ranking algorithms, which still consider the relevance and authority of back links.
- **User Experience**: PageRank aimed to improve the user experience by presenting more relevant and authoritative search results. By ranking pages based on their perceived importance within the web's interconnected structure, Google aimed to deliver higher-quality search results to users.

- **Influence on SEO**: Page Rank significantly influenced the SEO industry. Webmasters and SEO professionals focused on building high-quality back links to improve their websites' Page Rank and search engine rankings. While Page Rank is no longer the primary ranking factor, back links continue to be a crucial aspect of SEO.
- **Conceptual Basis**: The underlying idea of Page Rank—that the importance of a page can be determined by its connections to other important pages—has persisted in various forms. Today's search engines, including Google, use more complex algorithms that consider a wide range of factors, but the principle of evaluating a page's authority remains important.

It's worth noting that Google officially stopped updating the public Page Rank toolbar in 2016, signaling the decreasing significance of Page Rank as a publicly visible metric. While Page Rank may not be the dominant ranking factor it once was, it still influences the way search engines evaluate and rank web pages through more sophisticated algorithms that build on its foundational principles. As such, understanding the historical importance of Page Rank can contribute to a more comprehensive understanding of SEO and search engine technology.

Types of Google Page Rank:

Google Page Rank, often referred to as just Page Rank, was an algorithm developed by Larry Page and Sergey Brin, the founders of Google, to measure the importance or authority of web pages. It was a key component of Google's search ranking algorithm in its early years. Page Rank worked by assigning a numerical value (Page Rank score) to each web page based on the number and quality of links pointing to it. However, it's important to note that Google officially stopped updating and using Page Rank as a visible metric in 2016.

There were no different "types" of Page Rank, but there were different aspects and variations related to how PageRank worked and evolved. Here are some key points related to Page Rank:

- **Original Page Rank**: The original Page Rank algorithm calculated the importance of web pages based on the number and quality of back links they received. Pages with more high-quality back links were considered more important and received higher Page Rank scores.
- **Personalized Page Rank**: Google also used personalized Page Rank, which took into account the user's browsing history and behavior to deliver more personalized search results.
- **No follow Links:** Google introduced the "no follow" attribute for links, which allowed website owners to specify that certain links should not be considered when calculating Page Rank. This was done to combat spammy link building practices.
- **Toolbar Page Rank**: Google used to provide a Toolbar Page Rank metric that was visible to website owners and webmasters through a browser extension. However, this metric was discontinued in 2016, and Google no longer updates or uses it.
- **Internal Page Rank**: Page Rank wasn't just applied to external links; it was also used to measure the importance of internal pages within a website's structure. This helped determine the flow of Page Rank within a site.

- **Page Rank Sculpting**: Webmasters sometimes attempted to manipulate PageRank distribution within their websites by using no follow tags strategically. However, Google's algorithms evolved to prevent this practice from being effective.

It's important to emphasize that while Page Rank was a significant factor in Google's early search algorithm, Google has since moved to more complex and diverse ranking algorithms that take into account numerous other factors, such as content quality, user engagement, mobile-friendliness, and more. Therefore, while Page Rank played a crucial role in the history of search engine optimization (SEO), it is no longer the primary or sole determinant of a web page's ranking in Google's search results.

7.8 Steps to Increase Google Page Rank:

Increasing your website's Page Rank, a metric that was developed by Google to measure the importance of web pages, is not as relevant today as it once was. Google stopped updating Page Rank publicly in 2013, and it's no longer a primary factor in determining a website's ranking in search results. Instead, Google uses a complex algorithm that takes into account hundreds of factors to determine a page's ranking. Nevertheless, here are some general steps you can take to improve your website's visibility in search engine results:

- **High-Quality Content**: Create valuable, relevant, and high-quality content that addresses the needs and interests of your target audience. This should be your top priority.

- **Keyword Research**: Identify relevant keywords and phrases that people use to search for information related to your content. Use keyword research tools to find the best keywords to target.
- **On-Page SEO**: Optimize your website's on-page elements, including title tags, meta descriptions, headers, and image alt tags, to include your target keywords. Ensure that your content is well-structured and easy to read.
- **Mobile Optimization**: Make sure your website is mobile-friendly. Google prioritizes mobile-friendly websites in its rankings.
- **Page Speed**: Improve your website's loading speed. Faster websites tend to rank higher in search results. Use tools like Google Page Speed Insights to identify and fix speed issues.
- **Back links**: Although Page Rank is no longer publicly updated, back links (links from other websites to yours) are still a crucial ranking factor. Focus on building high-quality, relevant, and authoritative back links through guest posting, content marketing, and outreach.
- **Internal Links**: Create a logical internal linking structure within your website to help search engines understand the hierarchy and importance of your content.
- **User Experience (UX)**: Ensure that your website provides a positive user experience. This includes easy navigation, clear calls to action, and a visually appealing design.
- **Regular Updates**: Publish fresh content regularly, such as blog posts, articles, or news updates. Fresh content can attract both users and search engine crawlers.

- **Social Signals**: Engage with your audience on social media platforms. While social signals are not a direct ranking factor, they can indirectly influence your website's visibility.

Remember that SEO is an ongoing process, and it can take time to see significant improvements in your website's search engine rankings. Focus on providing value to your audience, and over time, you should see improvements in your online visibility.

Question: 7

1. Tell out about Off-page-SEO.?
2. What is mean by Off-Page optimization?
3. Summarize the Importance of Back links.?
4. Difference Between Do-Follow& No-Follow?
5. Illustrate the Meaning of Google page Rank.?
6. What are the Steps to Increase Page Rank?
7. Sketch about getting Backlines.?
8. What is mean by Off-Page & Off-Page Optimization?
9. Narrate about Search Engine Optimization.
10. Summarize about the importance of Backlines.
11. Compare between Do-Follow and No-Follow.
12. Tell about the meaning of Google page Rank.
13. Write the steps to increase Page Rank. And Explain in Detail.

CHAPTER - VIII

8.1 SEARCH ENGINE SUBMISSION:

Meaning:

Search engine submission refers to the process of submitting a website or web page to a search engine so that it can be included in the search engine's index or database. When a website is submitted to a search engine, it allows the search engine's crawlers or bots to discover and index the site's content, making it searchable by users when they enter relevant keywords in the search engine's query box.

Introduction:

Search engine submission refers to the process of submitting a website or webpage to search engines for indexing and inclusion in their search results. It is an essential step in the search engine optimization (SEO) process, as it helps search engines discover and catalog your website's content, making it accessible to users who are looking for relevant information or products online.

Here is an introduction to search engine submission:

1. **Purpose**: The primary purpose of search engine submission is to ensure that your website's pages are crawled and indexed by search engine bots. When your website is indexed, it becomes searchable on popular search engines like Google, Bing, Yahoo, and others.
2. **Visibility**: Submitting your website to search engines enhances its visibility. Without submission, search engines may eventually find your site, but the process could take

much longer. By proactively submitting your website, you expedite the indexing process.

3. **Indexing**: Search engine bots, also known as crawlers or spiders, continuously scan the web for new and updated content. When you submit your website, you are essentially informing these bots about your site's existence. They will then visit your website, analyze its content, and index it in their databases.
4. **Content Inclusion**: Search engine submission ensures that all your web pages are considered for inclusion in search engine results pages (SERPs). This is crucial for attracting organic traffic to your site.
5. **SEO Benefits**: Properly indexed and ranked web pages can appear in relevant search results, driving organic traffic to your website. This can lead to increased visibility, brand recognition, and potential revenue.
6. **Submission Methods**: Search engine submission can be done manually, by directly submitting your website's URL to each search engine's webmaster tools or submission forms. Alternatively, it can be automated through SEO tools and services, which can save time and effort.
7. **Best Practices**: While submitting your website, it's essential to follow best practices for SEO, such as optimizing your content, using relevant keywords, and ensuring that your website is mobile-friendly and loads quickly.
8. **Regular Updates**: Search engine submission is not a one-time process. It's essential to regularly update your website with fresh content and resubmit sitemaps to inform search engines of any changes.

9. **Diversification**: Don't focus solely on one search engine; submit your website to multiple search engines to reach a broader audience.
10. **Monitoring and Analytics**: After submission, use web analytics tools to track your website's performance in search results. Monitor your rankings and traffic to make informed SEO adjustments.

In summary, search engine submission is a crucial step in SEO that ensures your website is recognized, indexed, and ranked by search engines, ultimately leading to increased online visibility and potential business growth. However, it should be part of a broader SEO strategy that includes content optimization, link building, and ongoing monitoring and adjustments.

Overview of how search engine submission works:

1. **Website Creation**: First, a website is created with various web pages and content.
2. **Search Engine Submission**: The website owner or webmaster submits the website's URL (Uniform Resource Locator) or specific pages to search engines like Google, Bing, Yahoo, or others. This is typically done through the search engine's submission portal or webmaster tools.
3. **Crawling and Indexing**: Once the submission is made, search engine bots (also known as web crawlers or spiders) visit the submitted URLs to analyze the content and index it. They follow links within the website to discover additional pages.
4. **Search Results**: When users search for relevant keywords or phrases, the search engine's algorithm retrieves and

displays the indexed web pages in the search results. The pages are ranked based on various factors like relevance and quality.

It's important to note that in modern search engine optimization (SEO) practices, manual submission to search engines is less common and less necessary than it used to be. Search engines have become highly sophisticated at crawling and indexing websites on their own, especially for well-established and frequently updated sites. Webmasters can still use tools like Google Search Console or Bing Webmaster Tools to monitor their website's performance in search results and request re-crawling of specific pages if needed. However, simply submitting a site doesn't guarantee high search engine rankings; other SEO efforts like optimizing content and building high-quality backlinks are also crucial for improving search visibility.

8.2 Directory Submission Meaning:

Directory submission refers to the process of submitting a website or webpage's URL and related information to online directories or web directories. These directories are websites that organize and categorize links to other websites or WebPages. The goal of directory submission is to improve a website's online visibility and search engine rankings.

Here's how directory submission typically works:

1. **Selection of Directories**: Website owners or SEO professionals choose relevant and reputable online directories to submit their website to. These directories can be general or niche-specific, depending on the website's content or industry.

2. **Submission Information**: To submit a website, you usually need to provide information such as the website's URL, title, description, keywords, and sometimes additional details like your contact information or business address.
3. **Manual or Automated Submission:** Directory submissions can be done manually by visiting each directory's website and filling out the submission forms individually. Alternatively, there are automated directory submission tools or services that can streamline the process, but they may not always be recommended, as they can lead to low-quality submissions.
4. **Approval Process**: After submission, the directory's administrators review the information provided. If it meets their guidelines and standards, they may approve the listing and include it in their directory. However, not all submissions get approved, especially if the information provided is inaccurate, spammy, or not relevant to the directory's content.

Benefits of directory submission include:

1. **Improved Visibility:** Being listed in directories can help increase your website's visibility to potential visitors.
2. **Backlinks:** Many directories allow you to include a link to your website in the listing. These backlinks can potentially improve your website's search engine ranking.
3. **Niche Targeting:** Niche-specific directories can help you reach a more targeted audience interested in your industry or content.
4. **Local SEO**: Local business directories can be especially beneficial for businesses looking to improve their local search presence.

However, it's important to note that the impact of directory submissions on SEO has evolved over time. Search engines like Google have become more sophisticated and place a higher emphasis on the quality and relevance of backlinks. Low-quality directory submissions or excessive use of directory links without other SEO strategies may not yield significant results and could even harm your website's rankings if not done carefully.

In modern SEO practices, it's important to focus on high-quality, relevant directories and prioritize other SEO techniques such as creating valuable content, building natural backlinks, and optimizing your website for search engines. Directory submission should be part of a broader SEO strategy rather than the sole strategy.

Introduction:

Directory submission is a digital marketing and SEO (Search Engine Optimization) technique used to improve a website's online visibility and search engine rankings. It involves submitting your website's URL and relevant information to online directories or web directories. These directories are specialized websites that categorize and list various websites based on their niche or industry.

Here's an introduction to directory submission:

1. **Types of Directories:**

- **General Directories:** These directories cover a wide range of topics and categories.
- **Niche Directories:** These are focused on specific industries or topics, making them more targeted for relevant audiences.

- **Local Directories:** These directories concentrate on businesses and services within a specific geographical location.

2. **Benefits of Directory Submission:**

- **Improved Visibility:** Listing your website in directories makes it more accessible to users who browse these platforms.
- **Enhanced SEO:** Backlinks from reputable directories can boost your website's search engine rankings.
- **Targeted Traffic:** Niche and local directories can drive relevant traffic to your site, increasing the likelihood of conversions.
- **Credibility:** Being listed in authoritative directories can enhance your website's credibility and trustworthiness.

3. **How Directory Submission Works:**

- Research and select relevant directories based on your website's niche and target audience.
- Fill out submission forms with accurate and consistent information about your website, including its name, URL, description, keywords, and contact details.
- Some directories may require a reciprocal link, where you link back to their directory on your website.
- Review and adhere to the submission guidelines of each directory to ensure successful inclusion.

4. **Directory Submission Best Practices:**

- Choose reputable and high-quality directories to submit your website. Avoid spammy or low-quality directories.

- Use relevant keywords in your submissions to improve your website's chances of appearing in search results.
- Keep your directory listings up to date, especially if there are any changes to your website's information.

5. Directory Submission and SEO:

- While directory submissions can be beneficial for SEO, it's essential to diversify your backlink profile with other strategies like guest posting, social media, and content marketing.
- Overuse of directory submissions or relying solely on them for backlinks can lead to a penalty from search engines, so it's crucial to use them judiciously.

6. Tracking and Monitoring:

1. Keep track of the directories where you've submitted your website and regularly check for updates or changes in your listings.

- Monitor your website's performance in search results to assess the impact of directory submissions on your SEO efforts.

In conclusion, directory submission is a valuable tool in your digital marketing and SEO toolbox when used correctly. It can help increase your website's online presence, drive targeted traffic, and improve search engine rankings. However, it should be part of a broader SEO strategy that includes a variety of tactics to ensure long-term success.

8.3 Article Writing and Submission:

Meaning:

Article writing and submission refer to the process of creating written content and then sharing it with a specific audience or platform. This practice is commonly used in various contexts, including journalism, content marketing, academic research, and more. Here's a breakdown of what each term means:

1. **Article Writing:** This is the initial step in the process. Article writing involves creating written content on a specific topic, subject, or theme. The writer typically conducts research, organizes information, and crafts a well-structured and coherent piece of text. Articles can vary in length, style, and purpose, depending on the intended audience and platform.
2. **Article Submission:** After an article is written, it can be submitted to various platforms or publications for publication or dissemination. The goal of submission can vary based on the context:

- **Journalism:** Journalists submit articles to news outlets, magazines, or newspapers for publication. These articles are often intended to inform the public about current events, trends, or issues.
- **Content Marketing:** Businesses and content creators may submit articles to their websites, blogs, or third-party platforms to attract and engage their target audience. These articles can serve to educate, entertain, or promote products and services.
- **Academic Research:** Scholars and researchers submit articles to academic journals or conferences to share their

research findings with the academic community. These articles are typically peer-reviewed and contribute to the body of knowledge in a specific field.

- **Guest Posting:** Some writers submit articles to other websites or blogs as guest posts. This can help them reach a wider audience and establish themselves as experts in their field.

The process of submission often involves adhering to specific guidelines and requirements set by the platform or publication, including word count, formatting, and citation style. Once the article is submitted and approved, it becomes accessible to the target audience, whether it's the general public, a specific niche, or an academic community.

In the digital age, article submission has become more accessible through online platforms, blogs, social media, and content management systems. It allows individuals and organizations to share information, opinions, and expertise with a global audience, contributing to the exchange of knowledge and ideas.

Introduction of Article Writing and Submission :-

In the digital age, where information is readily available at our fingertips, article writing and submission have become indispensable tools for individuals and businesses alike. Whether you're a content creator, a marketer, or an expert in your field, the ability to craft compelling articles and distribute them effectively can have a significant impact on your online presence and reputation.

This article aims to explore the fundamental aspects of article writing and submission, highlighting their importance and providing valuable insights for those looking to harness the power of this dynamic medium. We will delve into the benefits of article writing and submission, discuss the key steps involved in crafting an engaging article, and offer strategies for effective distribution. By the end of this article, you will have a comprehensive understanding of how to leverage articles to convey your message, reach a wider audience, and establish yourself as a credible authority in your niche.

So, whether you're a seasoned writer looking to refine your skills or a business owner seeking to enhance your online visibility, read on to discover the world of article writing and submission and how it can be a game-changer for you

Article Writting and Submission Types:-

Article writing and submission are essential components of content marketing and online visibility strategies. They involve creating high-quality written content and then distributing it to various platforms for wider reach and exposure. There are several types of articles you can write and submit, each serving a different purpose. Here are some common types:

1. **Informative Articles:** These articles aim to educate and inform the reader about a specific topic. They provide valuable information, facts, and insights. Informative articles can cover a wide range of subjects, from how-to guides to in-depth explanations of complex concepts.
2. **News Articles:** News articles report on current events, developments, or trends within a particular industry or

field. They should be timely and objective, presenting the facts and providing context for readers.

3. **Opinion Pieces:** Also known as editorial articles, these pieces express the author's viewpoint on a particular issue. While they may be based on facts, opinion articles primarily present a subjective perspective and often invite discussion and debate.
4. **Listicles:** Listicles are articles structured as lists. They are popular because they are easy to read and offer information in a concise and organized manner. Examples include "10 Tips for Healthy Eating" or "Top 5 Travel Destinations."
5. **How-to Guides:** These articles provide step-by-step instructions on how to perform a specific task or achieve a particular goal. They are highly practical and can range from topics like "How to Start a Blog" to "How to Bake a Perfect Pie."
6. **Case Studies:** Case study articles examine real-life examples to illustrate a point or showcase the success of a product, service, or strategy. They often include data, testimonials, and in-depth analysis.
7. **Interviews:** Interview articles feature conversations with experts, influencers, or individuals with unique insights. They can provide valuable perspectives and offer a platform for sharing expertise.
8. **Product Reviews:** These articles evaluate and review products or services, providing readers with information to make informed purchasing decisions. They should be unbiased and include both pros and cons.

9. **Profiles:** Profile articles highlight a specific person, company, or organization, delving into their history, achievements, and contributions. They are often used for features on notable figures or businesses.
10. **Technical Papers:** Technical articles are highly specialized and cater to a specific audience with in-depth knowledge in a particular field. They often include technical jargon and detailed explanations.

When it comes to submitting articles, consider the following options:

1. **Guest Posting:** Contribute articles to websites or blogs in your niche or industry. Guest posting can help you reach a new audience and establish yourself as an authority.
2. **Content Platforms:** Publish articles on content platforms like Medium, LinkedIn, or WordPress. These platforms have built-in audiences and can increase your content's visibility.
3. **Article Directories:** Submit articles to article directories like EzineArticles, though their relevance and effectiveness have diminished over the years.
4. **Industry-specific Websites:** Many industries have specialized websites or publications that accept article submissions. Targeting these can help you reach a highly relevant audience.
5. **Press Releases:** Distribute press releases through services like PR Newswire or Business Wire to announce important news or developments related to your business.
6. **Social Media:** Share your articles on social media platforms to increase visibility and engagement. Encourage others to share your content as well.

7. **Email Newsletters:** If you have a mailing list, send your articles to your subscribers as part of your email marketing strategy.

Remember that regardless of the type of article you write or where you submit it, high-quality content that provides value to your target audience is key to a successful article marketing strategy.

8.4 Press Release and Writing and Submission:-

A press release is a written communication or statement issued by a company, organization, government agency, or individual to announce important news or information to the public, media outlets, and other interested parties. The primary purpose of a press release is to generate media coverage and public attention for a specific event, development, product launch, milestone, or any other newsworthy topic.

Writing a press release involves crafting a concise and informative document that conveys key details about the news you want to share. A well-written press release typically includes the following elements:

1. **Headline**: A clear and attention-grabbing title that summarizes the main point of the press release.
2. **Dateline:** The date and location of the press release, indicating when and where it was issued.
3. **Introduction/Lead**: A brief, compelling paragraph that provides the most important information and answers the "who," "what," "where," "when," "why," and "how" questions.

4. **Body:** One or more paragraphs that elaborate on the details of the news, providing additional context, background information, quotes, statistics, and other relevant facts.
5. **Quotes**: Including quotes from key figures involved in the news, such as company executives, spokespersons, or experts, can add credibility and a human touch to the release.
6. **Boilerplate:** A brief, standardized paragraph about the company, organization, or individual issuing the release, including relevant background information.
7. **Contact Information**: Details for a media contact person who can provide further information or arrange interviews.
8. **Call to Action:** Sometimes, a press release includes a call to action, encouraging readers to take specific steps, such as visiting a website, attending an event, or contacting the issuer for more information.
9. **Closing**: Indicating the end of the press release, often with the symbol "###" or "-END-."

Once a press release is written, the next step is submission. Press release submission involves distributing the release to various media outlets, journalists, bloggers, and other relevant parties. This can be done through several methods:

1. **Email:** Sending the press release directly to a list of media contacts or using press release distribution services that have established relationships with journalists.
2. **Wire Services**: Using press release distribution services like PR Newswire, Business Wire, or Marketwired to

disseminate the release to a wider audience of media professionals.

3. **Online Press Release Distribution**: Posting the press release on your own website or using online press release distribution platforms like PRWeb, PRLog, or Newswire to increase its online visibility.
4. **Social Media**: Sharing the press release on your organization's social media channels to reach a broader audience.
5. **Company Website**: Publishing the press release in the news or press section of your company's website so that it's easily accessible to interested parties.

Submitting a press release effectively is crucial for getting your news noticed and covered by the media, which can help you reach your target audience and achieve your communication goals.

Press Release and Writing and Submission Introduction

A press release is a valuable tool for businesses and organizations to share news and information with the public, media outlets, and stakeholders. Writing and submitting an effective press release can help generate publicity, increase brand visibility, and communicate important developments. Here's a step-by-step guide on how to write and submit a press release introduction:

1. **Understand Your Audience**: Before you begin writing, identify your target audience. Consider who would be interested in your news and tailor your message accordingly.

2. **Choose a Newsworthy Topic**: Your press release should focus on something newsworthy. This could be a product launch, a significant company milestone, an industry award, a major event, or any development that is relevant and interesting to your audience.
3. **Craft an Attention-Grabbing Headline**: The headline is the first thing readers see, so make it compelling and concise. Use active language and highlight the key point of your press release.
4. **Write a Subheadline (Optional)**: A subheadline can provide additional context or a brief summary of the press release. It's not always necessary but can be useful in certain cases.
5. **Write the Introduction:** The introduction is the first paragraph of your press release and should answer the essential questions: who, what, where, when, and why. It should provide a clear overview of the news you're sharing. Keep it concise and engaging.
6. **Include Supporting Details:** In the following paragraphs, provide more information about the news. Include relevant quotes from key individuals involved, statistics, and any other details that help to substantiate the importance of your announcement.
7. **Add Boilerplate Information**: Near the end of the press release, include a brief paragraph about your company or organization. This is known as the "boilerplate" and provides essential background information.
8. **Include Contact Information**: At the end of the press release, include contact details for a media contact person

who can answer questions or provide additional information.

9. **Use Associated Media:** If you have relevant images, videos, or infographics, include links or attachments that journalists can use to enhance their coverage.
10. **Formatting and Style**: Ensure your press release is well-formatted, with a clear structure. Use a professional tone and avoid jargon or excessive technical language. Check for grammar and spelling errors.
11. **Distribution:** Once your press release is ready, you can distribute it to various media outlets, journalists, and online press release distribution services. Consider using a newswire service or sending it directly to relevant reporters and editors.
12. **Follow Up:** After sending the press release, follow up with key contacts to gauge interest, answer questions, and provide additional information if needed.

Remember that the effectiveness of your press release depends on its relevance and the quality of your writing. Tailor each press release to the specific audience and news angle you're targeting, and be prepared to adapt your approach based on feedback and results.

Press Release and Writing and Submission Advantages :-

Press releases are powerful tools for businesses and organizations to communicate important information to the public, media outlets, and stakeholders. Writing and submitting press releases can offer several advantages, including:

1. **Visibility and Exposure**: Press releases can help increase your organization's visibility and exposure. When you distribute a well-written press release, it can be picked up by various media outlets, including newspapers, magazines, blogs, and news websites, giving your message a wide audience.
2. **Credibility:** A professionally written press release can enhance your organization's credibility and reputation. When your news is published by reputable media sources, it carries a certain level of trust and validation.
3. **SEO Benefits**: Press releases can improve your search engine optimization (SEO). When your press release is published online, it can include backlinks to your website, improving your website's authority and search engine ranking.
4. **Announcing News**: Press releases are an effective way to announce important news, such as product launches, company milestones, acquisitions, awards, or significant events. They provide a structured and concise format for sharing this information.
5. **Media Relations:** Press releases can help build and maintain positive relationships with media professionals. By providing them with newsworthy content in an accessible format, you make their job easier, increasing the likelihood that they will cover your story.
6. **Branding**: Consistent press releases can help reinforce your brand identity. By presenting your organization as a reliable source of information in your industry, you can build a strong brand image.

7. **Crisis Management:** In times of crisis or negative publicity, a well-crafted press release can be a tool for damage control. It allows you to address issues proactively and shape the narrative.
8. **Market Awareness**: Press releases can help potential customers and investors become aware of your products, services, and achievements. This can stimulate interest and drive sales or investment opportunities.
9. **Targeted Audience:** You can distribute press releases to specific audiences, tailoring your message to different groups, such as customers, investors, or industry insiders.
10. **Low-Cost Marketing**: Compared to traditional advertising methods, press releases are a cost-effective way to reach a broad audience. Many online distribution services offer affordable packages.
11. **Longevity**: Online press releases can remain accessible for an extended period, allowing people to discover your news even months after its initial publication.
12. **Analytics:** Most online press release distribution platforms provide analytics and tracking tools. This allows you to measure the impact of your press releases, including the number of views, shares, and clicks.
13. **Archiving**: Press releases can serve as a historical record of your organization's achievements and milestones, which can be valuable for future reference or documentation.

To maximize the advantages of press releases, it's crucial to invest in well-written, newsworthy content and to target the right audience through effective distribution channels. Additionally, maintaining a consistent press release strategy can help you build a strong online presence and brand reputation over time.

Press release and Writing and Submission Disadvantage :-

Press releases are a common tool used by businesses and organizations to share news and information with the media and the public. While they can be effective in some situations, they also have disadvantages:

6. **Limited Control over Message Interpretation:** Once a press release is submitted to the media, you have limited control over how the message is interpreted and presented to the public. Journalists may choose to focus on different aspects of the release or even alter the content to fit their editorial needs, potentially leading to a message that differs from your original intent.
7. **Saturation and Competition:** The media receives a large number of press releases daily. Yours may get lost in the shuffle, especially if it doesn't stand out or if there is significant competition for attention. This can result in your news not receiving the coverage you hoped for.
8. **Cost and Resource Investment:** Writing and distributing press releases can be time-consuming and may require financial resources if you hire a professional writer or use a distribution service. Smaller businesses and organizations may find this cost prohibitive.
9. **Lack of Guaranteed Coverage:** Submitting a press release does not guarantee that it will be picked up and covered by the media. Editors and journalists decide which stories to pursue based on their own criteria, and your news may not make the cut.
10. **Overuse and Skepticism:** Some media outlets and journalists have become skeptical of press releases due to their frequent use for marketing purposes. They may be

less likely to cover news that appears overly promotional or lacks genuine newsworthiness.

11. **One-Way Communication:** Press releases are essentially one-way communication. While they can disseminate information to the media and the public, they do not facilitate direct interaction or engagement with your target audience. In today's interactive digital age, two-way communication is often more effective for building relationships and trust.
12. **Risk of Misinterpretation:** There's always a risk that the message in your press release may be misinterpreted or taken out of context by the media or the public, which could lead to negative consequences for your organization.
13. **Limited Reach:** Press releases primarily target traditional media outlets, which may not reach all of your desired audience. In the age of social media and online communication, you may need additional strategies to reach a broader audience.
14. **Timing Challenges:** Timing is critical when it comes to press releases. If your release is not distributed at the right time or if it coincides with major news events, it may not receive the attention it deserves.
15. **Measurement and ROI:** Measuring the impact of a press release can be challenging. It's often difficult to quantify the return on investment (ROI) of a press release in terms of increased brand awareness, leads, or sales.

Despite these disadvantages, press releases can still be valuable for certain purposes, such as announcing major developments, crisis management, or when targeting specific industry publications. However, they should be used as part of a broader communication strategy that includes other channels like social media, content marketing, and direct engagement with your audience.

Blog Posting Meaning:

A blog post is a type of written content published on a blog, which is a website or online platform where individuals or organizations regularly share their thoughts, information, opinions, or experiences on a wide range of topics. Blog posts can vary in length and style but typically provide valuable or engaging information to readers.

Definition:

A blog post is a written or multimedia content piece published on a blog, which is a website or online platform where individuals or organizations regularly share information, ideas, opinions, and updates on various topics. Blog posts can cover a wide range of subjects, including personal experiences, hobbies, interests, news, reviews, tutorials, and more.

Typically, a blog post is structured with a title, introduction, main content body, and a conclusion. It can include text, images, videos, links, and other media to enhance the reader's understanding and engagement with the topic. Blog posts are often organized into categories or tagged with keywords to help readers navigate and find relevant content.

The purpose of a blog post can vary, such as informing, entertaining, educating, inspiring, or engaging with an audience. Blogging is a popular medium for individuals, businesses, and organizations to communicate with their audience, share their expertise, build a following, and even generate revenue through advertising, affiliate marketing, or selling products and services.

Characteristics of a blog post:

1. **Informative Content**: Blog posts often aim to inform, educate, or entertain readers. They can cover a wide array of subjects, such as technology, travel, fashion, health, cooking, and more.
2. **Personal Perspective**: Many blog posts are written from a personal perspective, allowing the author to share their unique viewpoint, experiences, and opinions on a particular subject.
3. **Varied Formats**: Blog posts can take various formats, including how-to guides, listicles, opinion pieces, reviews, interviews, and personal stories.
4. **Regular Updates**: Blogs typically feature a series of regularly updated posts, with new content being added over time. This allows bloggers to engage their audience consistently.
5. **Interaction:** Blog posts often encourage reader interaction through comments, likes, shares, and social media links. This interaction can create a sense of community around the blog.
6. **Multimedia Elements:** Blog posts may include images, videos, infographics, and other multimedia elements to enhance the content and make it more engaging.

7. **SEO Considerations**: Bloggers often optimize their posts for search engines (SEO) to increase the visibility of their content in search results, attracting more readers.
8. **Archives:** Older blog posts are typically archived on the blog, making it easy for readers to access past content.
9. **Categories and Tags**: Blog posts are often categorized and tagged to help readers navigate the blog and find content relevant to their interests.
10. **Publishing Platform**: Blog posts are usually created and published using blogging platforms such as Word Press, Blogger, Medium, or custom-built websites with blogging functionality.

Blog posts serve various purposes, including sharing knowledge, building an online presence, promoting products or services, expressing creativity, and connecting with a target audience. They are a fundamental component of the blogging medium and have contributed significantly to the democratization of online content creation and dissemination.

Content Writing Meaning:

Content writing refers to the process of creating written material for various purposes and platforms, such as websites, blogs, social media, marketing materials, and more. The primary goal of content writing is to engage, inform, or persuade a target audience by delivering valuable and relevant information.

Content Writing Definition:

Content writing is the process of creating written material for various digital or print platforms, with the primary goal of conveying information, engaging an audience, or promoting a product, service, or idea. Content writing encompasses a wide range of formats, including articles, blog posts, web pages, social media posts, product descriptions, email newsletters, whitepapers, eBooks, and more.

Effective content writing not only involves delivering information accurately but also focuses on making the content engaging, informative, and tailored to the needs and interests of the target audience. It often requires research, proper structuring, and attention to grammar, spelling, and style to ensure clarity and readability.

Content writers often work in various industries and sectors, such as marketing, journalism, blogging, technical writing, and academia. They play a crucial role in online marketing strategies, as high-quality content can attract and retain readers, improve search engine rankings, and establish authority and credibility in a particular field.

Content writers typically produce written content that can take various forms, including:

1. **Blog Posts:** Articles written for blogs to inform, educate, or entertain readers on specific topics.
2. **Website Content:** Textual content found on webpages, including homepage content, product descriptions, and About Us pages.
3. **Social Media Posts:** Captions, status updates, and other text-based content shared on social media platforms.
4. **Product Descriptions:** Detailed information about products or services to help potential customers make informed decisions.

5. **Email Marketing:** Creating compelling email content for newsletters, promotional campaigns, and customer communication.
6. **Press Releases:** Announcements and news articles to inform the public and media about important developments.
7. **Whitepapers and eBooks:** In-depth documents that provide valuable information on a specific subject.
8. **Copywriting:** Writing persuasive and attention-grabbing text for advertisements, sales pages, and marketing materials.

Effective content writing involves understanding the target audience, using appropriate language and tone, conducting research to ensure accuracy and credibility, and optimizing content for search engines (SEO) when necessary. The goal is to create content that resonates with the intended audience, delivers value, and achieves the desired communication objectives.

Comment Writing Definition:

Comment writing, in a general context, refers to the act of composing a brief text or message to express thoughts, opinions, feedback, or reactions in response to something. These comments can be written in various forms, including online comments on websites, social media platforms, blog posts, articles, or even handwritten notes on physical documents. Comment writing serves as a means of communication, engagement, and interaction, allowing individuals to participate in discussions, provide feedback, ask questions, or share their perspectives on a wide range of topics and content.

The purposes of comment writing can vary widely and may include:

1. **Feedback:** Providing constructive criticism or positive feedback on a product, service, or piece of content.
2. **Discussion:** Engaging in a conversation or debate with others to exchange ideas and viewpoints.
3. **Information Sharing:** Sharing additional information or insights related to the topic being discussed.
4. **Support:** Offering encouragement, empathy, or support to individuals who may be going through a challenging situation or seeking advice.
5. **Community Building:** Fostering a sense of community and connection by interacting with others who share similar interests or concerns.
6. **Validation:** Expressing agreement or validation with the content or opinions presented.
7. **Questioning:** Asking questions to seek clarification or gather more information.

Effective comment writing often involves clarity, respect for others, and adherence to any guidelines or etiquette established in the particular platform or context. Meaningful comments can contribute to productive discussions and enhance the overall quality of online and offline interactions.

Comment Writing Types:

Writing can be categorized into various types or genres, each with its own unique characteristics and purposes. Here are some common writing types:

1. **Narrative Writing**: This type of writing tells a story. It can be fiction or non-fiction and often includes characters,

settings, and a plot. Novels, short stories, autobiographies, and memoirs are examples of narrative writing.

2. **Descriptive Writing**: Descriptive writing aims to paint a vivid picture for the reader by using sensory details. It is often used in poetry, travel writing, and creative non-fiction to create a strong sense of place or emotion.
3. **Expository Writing**: Expository writing is informative and objective. Its purpose is to explain, inform, or instruct. Examples include essays, research papers, news articles, and textbooks.
4. **Persuasive Writing:** Persuasive writing is meant to convince the reader to adopt a particular viewpoint or take a specific action. It's often used in advertisements, editorials, speeches, and opinion pieces.
5. **Argumentative Writing**: Similar to persuasive writing, argumentative writing presents a clear argument or thesis and supports it with evidence and logical reasoning. It is common in academic essays and debates.
6. **Poetry:** Poetry is a form of artistic writing that often uses rhyme, meter, and metaphor to convey emotions, ideas, or stories. It comes in various styles and forms, such as sonnets, haikus, and free verse.
7. **Technical Writing**: Technical writing is precise and aims to convey complex information in a clear and concise manner. It's common in manuals, user guides, scientific papers, and reports.
8. **Journalistic Writing:** Journalistic writing is focused on reporting news and events. It follows a specific style, with the most important information presented at the beginning (inverted pyramid style). News articles and features fall into this category.

9. **Creative Writing**: This is a broad category that encompasses various forms of imaginative and artistic writing. It includes fiction, poetry, creative non-fiction, and more. Creative writers often prioritize artistic expression and originality.
10. **Business Writing**: Business writing is used in professional settings to communicate within and outside an organization. It includes emails, memos, reports, proposals, and business letters.
11. **Academic Writing:** Academic writing is used in educational settings and focuses on research, analysis, and critical thinking. It includes essays, research papers, theses, and dissertations.
12. **Blogging**: Blogging is a digital form of writing where individuals or organizations create online content on various topics. Blog posts can vary in style and purpose, from personal diaries to informational articles.
13. **Social Media Writing**: Writing for social media platforms involves crafting concise and engaging content for platforms like Twitter, Facebook, Instagram, and LinkedIn. It often includes hashtags, emojis, and multimedia elements.

These are just some of the many types of writing that exist. Writers often specialize in one or more of these forms, depending on their interests, skills, and goals. Each type of writing requires its own set of techniques and approaches to effectively convey the intended message or achieve its purpose.

Classifieds Posting:

Meaning:

Classifieds posting refers to the act of creating and publishing advertisements or listings in classified advertising sections, both in print and online media, to promote products, services, or job opportunities. Classified ads are typically organized into specific categories such as "For Sale," "Services," "Jobs," "Real Estate," and more, making it easier for individuals or businesses to find and search for what they are looking for.

In the context of online classifieds, websites and platforms like Craigslist, Gumtree, and various social media marketplaces allow users to post classified ads to reach a wider audience. These ads often contain essential information such as a brief description of the item or service, contact details, and sometimes a price.

Classifieds postings are a popular way for individuals and businesses to buy, sell, trade, or advertise their offerings to a specific target audience, making it a valuable tool for marketing and connecting with potential customers or clients.

Definition:

Classifieds posting refers to the act of creating and publishing advertisements or listings in classified advertising platforms, newspapers, websites, or other media outlets. These advertisements typically provide information about products, services, job openings, housing, or other offerings in a structured format. Classified ads are organized into specific categories or sections, making it easier for potential buyers, sellers, or job seekers to find relevant information.

The key elements of a classified ad typically include:

1. **Title:** A concise and attention-grabbing headline that summarizes the main offering or purpose of the ad.
2. **Description:** A detailed description of the product, service, job, or housing opportunity being advertised. This section provides essential information to potential buyers, such as features, specifications, and pricing.
3. **Contact Information**: Contact details for the person or business placing the ad, such as a phone number, email address, or location.
4. **Category:** The ad is typically placed in a specific category that best matches the nature of the offering, such as "For Sale," "Jobs," "Housing," "Services," or "Personals."
5. **Pricing:** For ads related to items for sale or services, the price or pricing details are often included.
6. **Location:** In housing and job ads, the location of the property or job position is important information.
7. **Images:** Some classified ads may include images or photos to provide visual representation of the product, service, or property being advertised.
8. **Duration:** The period for which the ad will be active or the publication date may also be specified.

Classified ads are widely used for various purposes, such as buying and selling items, finding employment opportunities, renting or selling real estate, promoting services, and more. They are a common way for individuals and businesses to reach a targeted audience and connect with potential customers or clients. Classified advertising platforms can be found both online and in print publications, and they serve as a convenient and organized way for people to browse and search for specific offerings or opportunities.

Forum Posting Meaning:

Forum posting refers to the act of participating in online discussion forums or message boards by posting messages, comments, or responses to existing discussions or starting new threads on various topics. These forums are usually hosted on websites dedicated to specific subjects, interests, or communities, and they provide a platform for people to interact, share information, ask questions, and engage in conversations with others who have similar interests or concerns.

Forum postings can take various forms, including text-based messages, links to external content, images, and sometimes even multimedia content. Participants in forums are typically referred to as "users" or "members," and they may use usernames or pseudonyms to protect their privacy or establish a unique online identity.

Forum posting serves several purposes, including:

1. **Sharing Information:** Users can share their knowledge, experiences, and expertise on specific topics to help others learn or solve problems.
2. **Asking Questions:** Users can seek advice, ask questions, and request information from the forum community to gain insights or solutions to their queries.
3. **Engaging in Discussions:** Users can participate in ongoing conversations, debates, or discussions related to their interests.
4. **Building Community:** Forums often foster a sense of community among like-minded individuals who share common interests or concerns.

5. **Networking:** Users can connect with others who have similar interests, which can lead to valuable connections in personal or professional life.
6. **Promoting Content:** Some users may use forums to share their own content, such as blog posts, articles, or products, within the guidelines of the forum's rules and policies.

It's important to note that different forums may have specific rules and guidelines governing behavior, such as rules against spamming, trolling, or engaging in inappropriate or offensive discussions. Participants are expected to adhere to these rules to maintain a positive and constructive environment within the forum community.

Definition of Forum Posting:

Forum posting refers to the act of participating in online discussion forums or message boards by posting comments, questions, or responses to existing discussions. These forums are typically organized around specific topics or interests, and they provide a platform for individuals to engage in conversations, share information, seek advice, or express their opinions on various subjects.

Forum posting can take many forms, including:

1. **Creating New Threads:** Users can start new discussions by creating a new thread or topic. They typically provide a title and a message to initiate a conversation on a particular subject.
2. **Replying to Existing Threads:** Users can join ongoing discussions by posting replies or comments in response to existing threads. They can share their thoughts, answer

questions, or provide additional information related to the topic at hand.

3. **Asking Questions:** Forums are often used as a place to seek answers to specific questions. Users can post queries in relevant sections of the forum and wait for other members to respond with helpful information.
4. **Sharing Information:** Individuals can use forum posting to share their knowledge, experiences, or resources with others who have similar interests or concerns. This could involve providing tips, guides, or recommendations.
5. **Engaging in Discussions:** Forum posting allows users to engage in meaningful discussions with like-minded individuals or those who hold different viewpoints. It can involve debates, brainstorming sessions, or just casual conversations.
6. **Networking:** Some people use forums as a means of networking with others who share their professional or personal interests. This can lead to valuable connections and collaborations.

Forum posting can be a valuable way to exchange information, seek assistance, and connect with people who share your interests. It's important to follow the specific rules and guidelines of each forum and to maintain a respectful and constructive tone when participating in these online communities.

Components of Forum Posting:

Forum posting typically involves several components to create a meaningful and effective contribution to an online discussion forum. Here are the key components:

1. **Title/Subject:** Your post should have a clear and descriptive title that summarizes the topic or question you want to discuss. It should grab the reader's attention and provide a preview of the content.
2. **Body/Content:** The body of your forum post contains the main content of your message. It should be well-structured and organized, with clear and concise writing. Here's what you should include in the body:

- **Introduction:** Begin with a brief introduction to the topic or issue you're addressing. Explain why it's important or interesting.
- **Main Content:** Provide detailed information, arguments, or explanations related to your topic. Use paragraphs and headings if necessary to make the content more readable.
- **Supporting Evidence:** Back up your points with relevant facts, data, examples, or references to authoritative sources. This adds credibility to your post.
- **Questions or Discussion Points:** If you have specific questions or want to foster discussion, pose them clearly within your post. This encourages other forum members to engage with your topic.
- **Personal Experience:** Share your personal experiences or anecdotes if they are relevant to the discussion. This can make your post more relatable.
- **Conclusion:** Summarize your main points or provide a conclusion to your post. This helps readers understand the key takeaways.

3. **Formatting:** Use formatting options provided by the forum (e.g., bold, italics, bullet points, numbering) to emphasize important information, create lists, or make

your post more visually appealing. Proper formatting makes your post easier to read.

4. **Links and References:** If you're citing external sources, include hyperlinks to those sources when possible. Make sure to follow the forum's rules regarding the inclusion of links.
5. **Images or Media:** If visuals are relevant to your topic, consider including images, videos, or other media to enhance your post. Ensure you have the right to use and share any media you include.
6. **Signature:** Some forums allow users to have a signature block at the end of their posts. This is a brief section where you can include information about yourself, your website, or contact details if permitted by the forum's rules.
7. **Tags and Categories:** Assign appropriate tags or categories to your post to help other users find it easily within the forum's structure.
8. **Spelling and Grammar:** Proofread your post to eliminate errors in spelling and grammar. Well-written posts are more likely to be taken seriously.
9. **Respectful Tone:** Maintain a respectful and courteous tone throughout your post, even if you disagree with others. Avoid offensive language, personal attacks, or inflammatory comments.
10. **Engagement:** After posting, actively engage with other forum members by responding to comments, answering questions, and participating in the discussion. This helps build a sense of community and credibility.
11. **Review Forum Rules:** Familiarize yourself with the specific rules and guidelines of the forum you're using.

Different forums may have different posting requirements and etiquette.

By including these components in your forum posts, you can contribute effectively to discussions and engage with other members of the online community in a meaningful way.

Business Listing:

A business listing refers to a public online profile or directory entry that provides information about a specific business, such as its name, address, phone number, website, operating hours, and a brief description of its products or services. These listings can be found on various online platforms, including search engines, social media networks, review sites, and specialized business directories.

Business listings serve several purposes:

1. **Visibility:** They make it easier for potential customers to find and contact a business. When someone searches for a product or service online, having a well-maintained business listing can increase the chances of your business appearing in search results.
2. **Credibility:** A complete and accurate business listing can build trust with potential customers. It shows that your business is legitimate and provides essential contact information.
3. **SEO (Search Engine Optimization):** Optimizing your business listings can improve your website's search engine rankings. Consistent and accurate information across various online platforms can boost your online presence.

4. **Accessibility:** Business listings make it convenient for customers to get in touch with your business, whether they're looking for your phone number, address, or operating hours.
5. **Reviews and Ratings:** Some business listings platforms allow customers to leave reviews and ratings. These can influence potential customers' decisions and provide valuable feedback for your business.

Business listings are commonly found on platforms like Google My Business, Yelp, Facebook Pages, Yellow Pages, and industry-specific directories. Managing and maintaining accurate business listings is an essential part of online marketing and reputation management for businesses of all sizes.

Social Bookmarking:

Social bookmarking is a method of saving, organizing, and sharing web pages, articles, videos, and other online content for future reference or for sharing with others. It is typically done through online platforms or websites designed for this purpose. Here's how it works:

1. **Bookmarking:** Users can add bookmarks (links) to web pages they find interesting or useful. These bookmarks are often accompanied by tags or keywords that describe the content, making it easier to categorize and search for later.
2. **Social Sharing:** The "social" aspect comes into play when users share their bookmarks with others. This can be done by making bookmarks public, allowing others to view and access the saved links, or by sharing them with specific individuals or groups within the platform.

3. **Discovering Content:** Users can explore and discover content that other people have bookmarked. This can help them find valuable resources, articles, websites, or videos that align with their interests.
4. **Collaboration:** Some social bookmarking platforms allow for collaboration and discussion around the saved content. Users can comment on bookmarks, vote on their usefulness, or even collaborate on shared collections of bookmarks.
5. **Organization:** Social bookmarking platforms often provide tools for organizing bookmarks into folders or categories, making it easier to manage a large collection of links.

Popular social bookmarking platforms in the past included Delicious and StumbleUpon, but the landscape has evolved, and many people now use general social media platforms or browser extensions for bookmarking and sharing content. Nonetheless, the fundamental concept of saving and sharing online resources remains the same. Social bookmarking can be a valuable tool for individuals and groups looking to curate and share content relevant to their interests or work.

Introduction about Bookmarking:

Bookmarks are a simple yet indispensable tool for readers, serving as a means to mark and easily return to specific pages or sections within a book, magazine, or any printed material. They provide a convenient way to keep track of your progress, highlight key passages, or organize your reading experience. Beyond their practical utility, bookmarks can also carry personal and aesthetic significance, often reflecting the reader's taste and personality.

In the digital age, the concept of bookmarking has expanded to encompass a wide range of digital content, including web pages, e-books, and multimedia files. Digital bookmarks serve the same fundamental purpose as their physical counterparts, allowing users to save and revisit digital resources, websites, or media at a later time with ease.

Bookmarks play a pivotal role in enhancing reading and research experiences, enabling efficient navigation through vast amounts of information. Whether in the tangible form of a folded page corner or the digital form of a clickable link, bookmarks continue to be an essential tool for readers and information seekers alike. This enduring practice of bookmarking underscores its enduring relevance in an ever-evolving world of information consumption.

Social Networking RSS:

The term "Social Networking RSS" does not have a standard or widely recognized meaning. However, I can break down the components of this phrase to help you understand its possible implications:

1. **Social Networking**: Social networking refers to the use of websites, apps, or platforms that enable individuals to connect and interact with others online. Popular social networking platforms include Facebook, Twitter, Instagram, LinkedIn, and many others. Users typically create profiles, share content, connect with friends or colleagues, and engage in various forms of communication within these networks.

2. **RSS**: RSS stands for "Really Simple Syndication" or "Rich Site Summary." It is a web feed technology used to publish frequently updated content, such as blog posts, news articles, podcasts, and more, in a standardized format. Users can subscribe to RSS feeds to receive updates from their favorite websites or sources without visiting each site individually. RSS readers or aggregators help users organize and read this content.

When combined, "Social Networking RSS" could potentially refer to a concept or tool that integrates RSS feeds with social networking platforms. This integration might allow users to share RSS feed content with their social network contacts, automatically post updates from RSS feeds to their social media profiles, or create a more streamlined way to consume and share content from both sources. However, without a specific context or product with this name, it's challenging to provide a precise definition.

If you have a specific context or application in mind related to "Social Networking RSS," please provide more details, and I can offer a more tailored explanation

Importance of Social Networking RSS:

Social networking and RSS (Really Simple Syndication) serve different but complementary purposes in the digital world. Let's explore the importance of each and how they relate:

1. **Social Networking Importance:** Social networking platforms like Facebook, Twitter, Instagram, LinkedIn, and others are vital for various reasons:

- **Connectivity**: They enable people to connect with friends, family, colleagues, and communities worldwide, fostering communication and relationships.
- **Information Sharing**: Users can share their thoughts, opinions, updates, and multimedia content, allowing for real-time information dissemination.
- **Marketing and Promotion**: Businesses use social networks to reach their target audience, advertise products/services, and engage with customers.
- **Trends and Virality**: Social media can quickly spread trends, news, and viral content, influencing public opinion and behavior.
- **Engagement and Interaction**: It provides a platform for engaging discussions, debates, and interactions on various topics.

2. **RSS Importance:** RSS is a web feed format used to syndicate content from websites and blogs. Its importance lies in several aspects:

- **Content Aggregation**: RSS allows users to aggregate content from multiple sources into a single feed. This is useful for keeping up with news, blogs, podcasts, and other online content without visiting each website individually.
- **Efficiency**: RSS saves time by delivering updates in one place, reducing the need to check multiple websites manually.
- **Privacy**: RSS does not require personal information or user accounts, which can be appealing to individuals concerned about privacy.

- **Customization**: Users can choose the specific sources and topics they want to follow, tailoring their content consumption.
- **Professional Use**: RSS feeds are essential for content syndication on websites, enabling automatic updates of news or blog sections.

3. **Relationship Between Social Networking and RSS:** While they serve different purposes, there's a connection between social networking and RSS:

- **Content Sharing**: Social networks often use RSS feeds to automatically share content from blogs or websites, ensuring that users stay updated with the latest posts from their favorite sources.
- **Content Promotion**: Social media platforms can be used to promote RSS feeds, encouraging users to subscribe to their preferred content sources.
- **Content Discovery**: Users can discover new websites and blogs through social networking recommendations or by following influencers who share RSS feeds.

In summary, social networking and RSS have their unique roles in the digital landscape. Social networking platforms focus on communication, engagement, and real-time updates, while RSS simplifies content aggregation and distribution. Their importance depends on individual preferences and needs, with some users relying heavily on social networks for daily interactions and others using RSS to manage and consume specific content efficiently

Significance of Social Networking RSS:

Social networking and RSS (Really Simple Syndication) are two distinct but interconnected concepts in the realm of online communication and content distribution. Let's explore the significance of each and how they can be related:

1. **Social Networking**:

- **Connectivity**: Social networking platforms like Facebook, Twitter, Instagram, LinkedIn, etc., have revolutionized the way people connect and communicate online. They allow individuals to create profiles, connect with friends and colleagues, and share various types of content, including text, images, videos, and links.
- **Global Reach**: Social networking has a global reach, enabling individuals and businesses to connect with a diverse and broad audience. This global reach is significant for personal communication, marketing, brand promotion, and even activism.
- **User-Generated Content**: Social networks thrive on user-generated content. Users create and share content with their networks, contributing to the platform's content ecosystem. This content can be personal updates, news articles, product reviews, and more.

2. **RSS (Really Simple Syndication)**:

- **Content Distribution**: RSS is a technology that allows content publishers (websites, blogs, news outlets) to syndicate their content in a standardized format. Users can subscribe to RSS feeds to receive updates from their favorite sources automatically.

- **Efficiency**: RSS helps users aggregate content from multiple sources in one place, called an RSS reader. This simplifies the process of staying updated on various topics and eliminates the need to visit each website individually.
- **Customization**: RSS allows users to tailor their content consumption by subscribing to specific feeds. This customization ensures that users receive content that aligns with their interests.

Significance of Combining Social Networking and RSS:

- **Content Sharing**: Many social networking platforms integrate RSS feeds or allow users to share content from RSS feeds. This integration makes it easy for users to share articles, blog posts, or news updates with their social network connections.
- **Discovery and Engagement**: RSS can help users discover new content and sources of information. When individuals share RSS-fed content on social media, it can lead to discussions, engagement, and the dissemination of valuable information.
- **Content Curation**: Social networking platforms often provide tools for users to curate and share collections of content. RSS can be a valuable source for curating content that's relevant to a user's niche or interests.

In summary, the significance of social networking lies in its ability to connect people, share user-generated content, and facilitate global communication. RSS, on the other hand, simplifies content distribution and consumption. Combining the two can enhance content discovery, sharing, and engagement on social media platforms, making it easier for users to stay informed and share valuable content with their networks

Fees Do's and Dont's of Link Building:

Link building is an essential aspect of search engine optimization (SEO) that involves acquiring hyperlinks from other websites to your own. When done correctly, it can help improve your website's visibility in search engine results and drive more organic traffic. However, there are some important do's and don'ts to keep in mind to ensure that your link-building efforts are effective and adhere to search engine guidelines:

Do's of Link Building:

1. **Create High-Quality Content:** The foundation of successful link building is creating valuable and relevant content that others want to link to. Quality content naturally attracts links.
2. **Guest Blogging:** Write high-quality guest posts for reputable websites in your industry. Ensure the content is informative and adds value to the audience.
3. **Outreach:** Reach out to website owners and influencers in your niche to establish relationships and request backlinks. Personalized and genuine outreach is key.
4. **Use Social Media:** Share your content on social media platforms to increase its visibility. Engage with your audience to encourage them to share your content as well.
5. **Internal Linking:** Incorporate internal links within your website to connect related content. This helps with user experience and SEO.
6. **Directory Listings:** Submit your website to relevant and trustworthy online directories, such as Google My Business and industry-specific directories.

7. **Collaborate:** Partner with other websites or businesses for co-marketing efforts, such as co-authored content or events.

Don'ts of Link Building:

1. **Avoid Buying Links:** Purchasing links or engaging in link schemes is against search engine guidelines and can result in penalties. Focus on organic, earned links.
2. **Low-Quality Guest Posting:** Don't contribute low-quality or irrelevant guest posts to websites solely for the purpose of getting a link. Google is keen on detecting and penalizing this practice.
3. **Over-Optimized Anchor Text:** Using the same exact keyword-rich anchor text repeatedly in your links can look unnatural and trigger penalties. Vary your anchor text with natural phrases.
4. **Link Farms and PBNs:** Avoid participating in or associating with link farms (websites designed solely for link building) and private blog networks (PBNs). These are considered black hat tactics.
5. **Irrelevant Links:** Don't get links from websites that are unrelated to your niche or industry. Links should be contextually relevant.
6. **Neglecting User Experience:** Ensure that the links you place within your content don't disrupt the user experience. They should enhance, not detract from, the user's journey.
7. Ignoring Analytics: Regularly monitor the performance of your links using analytics tools. Remove or disavow low-quality or toxic back links that could harm your SEO.

8. **Ignoring No follow Links:** While Do follow links pass SEO value, nofollow links (when used properly) can still drive traffic and enhance your link profile diversity.

Remember that link building is a long-term strategy, and patience is key. Focus on building natural, high-quality links that benefit your audience and your website's SEO. Avoid shortcuts and tactics that can harm your website's reputation and rankings in the long run.

Easy Link acquisition Techniques :-

"Easy link acquisition techniques" refer to relatively straightforward methods or strategies for obtaining backlinks to a website. Backlinks, also known as inbound links or incoming links, are links from other websites that point to your site. They are crucial for search engine optimization (SEO) because search engines like Google consider them when determining a website's authority and relevance.

Here are some easy link acquisition techniques, along with a brief explanation of each:

1. **Guest Blogging:** Write high-quality articles for other websites in your niche, including a link back to your site in your author bio or within the content itself.
2. **Directory Submissions:** Submit your website to reputable online directories and business listings. Ensure that you choose directories relevant to your industry or location.
3. **Social Media Profiles:** Create and optimize social media profiles for your business or website, and include links to your site in the profiles.

4. **Forum Participation:** Engage in relevant online forums and communities by providing valuable input and including a link to your site in your forum signature, if allowed.
5. Blog Comments: Leave thoughtful and relevant comments on blog posts in your niche, and include a link back to your site in the comment if it adds value to the discussion.
6. **Content Sharing:** Share your website's content on social media platforms, content aggregators, and social bookmarking sites.
7. **Broken Link Building:** Identify broken or outdated links on other websites in your niche, and reach out to the site owner suggesting your content as a replacement link.
8. **Email Outreach:** Contact other website owners or bloggers in your industry and propose collaboration opportunities or request guest posting opportunities with back links.
9. **Link Reclamation:** Monitor mentions of your brand or website online and reach out to website owners who have mentioned you but haven't linked to your site. Request them to add a link to your website.
10. **Resource Pages:** Find websites with resource or links pages in your niche and request to be added to these pages if your content is relevant and valuable.
11. **Local Citations:** Ensure that your business information is accurate and consistent across online directories and local business listings.
12. **Partnerships:** Collaborate with other businesses or websites in your industry for joint promotions or content sharing, which may include back links.

It's important to note that while these techniques can help you acquire back links, the quality of the links and their relevance to your website's content and audience matter more than quantity. High-quality, relevant back links from authoritative websites are more valuable in terms of SEO than a large number of low-quality links. Additionally, always prioritize ethical and white-hat SEO practices to ensure your website's long-term success

Domain Authority Meaning:

Domain Authority (DA) is a metric developed by Moz, a software company that specializes in SEO (Search Engine Optimization) tools. DA is used to assess the overall authority or credibility of a website in search engines. It's measured on a scale from 1 to 100, with higher scores indicating greater authority and a better potential for ranking well in search engine results.

Several factors influence a website's Domain Authority, including:

1. **Backlinks:** The number and quality of backlinks (links from other websites to your site) play a significant role in determining DA. High-quality, authoritative backlinks from reputable websites tend to boost a site's DA.
2. **Content Quality:** The quality and relevance of the content on a website can impact its DA. High-quality, informative, and well-structured content tends to attract more backlinks and improve a site's authority.
3. **Site Age:** Older websites generally have higher DA scores because they have had more time to accumulate backlinks and establish authority.

4. **Technical SEO:** Proper technical optimization of a website, including factors like site speed, mobile-friendliness, and clean code, can contribute to higher Domain Authority.
5. **Social Signals:** While not as influential as other factors, social signals (engagement and sharing on social media) can have a small impact on DA.

It's important to note that Domain Authority is a relative metric, meaning it should be used to compare websites within the same niche or industry rather than across all websites on the internet. A DA score of 20 might be considered high in a niche with low competition, while the same score would be considered low in a highly competitive niche.

Webmasters and SEO professionals use Domain Authority as one of many metrics to assess the strength of a website's online presence and its potential for ranking well in search engine results. However, it's not a direct factor used by search engines like Google in determining search rankings; it's a tool developed by Moz to help webmasters make informed decisions about their SEO efforts.

How to Increase Domain Authority:

Increasing Domain Authority (DA) is a long-term process that involves improving the overall authority and credibility of your website in the eyes of search engines like Google. Domain Authority is a metric developed by Moz that measures the relative strength of a website's back link profile and can influence its search engine ranking. Here are some strategies to help you increase your Domain Authority:

1. **Quality Content Creation:**

- Create high-quality, valuable, and informative content that resonates with your target audience. This can include blog posts, articles, videos, info graphics, and more.

2. **On-Page SEO:**

- Optimize your content for relevant keywords and phrases. Ensure proper use of headings, meta tags, alt tags, and a clear website structure.

3. **Technical SEO:**

- Ensure your website is technically sound. This includes optimizing page load times, fixing broken links, ensuring mobile-friendliness, and having a secure HTTPS connection.

4. **Backlink Building:**

- Focus on acquiring high-quality back links from reputable websites in your niche. Guest posting, influencer outreach, and content promotion can help with this.

5. **Social Media Engagement:**

- Be active on social media platforms and share your content. Social signals can indirectly impact your DA.

6. **Internal Linking:**

- Properly structure and use internal links to connect related content within your website. This can help distribute authority throughout your site.

7. **Remove Toxic Back links:**
- Regularly monitor your back link profile and disavow or remove toxic or spammy back links that can harm your DA.

8. **User Experience (UX):**
- Improve the overall user experience of your website, including navigation, mobile optimization, and page speed.

9. **Mobile Optimization:**
- Ensure your website is responsive and optimized for mobile devices, as Google places a significant emphasis on mobile-friendliness.

10. **Consistency and Patience:**
- Increasing DA takes time. Consistently apply these strategies, and over time, you should see improvements.

11. **Quality Over Quantity:**
- It's better to have a few high-quality back links from authoritative sources than numerous low-quality links.

12. **Competitor Analysis:**
- Analyze your competitors with higher DAs and see what strategies they are using. This can provide insights into what works in your industry.

13. **Content Promotion:**
- Promote your content through various channels, such as email marketing, social media, and influencer outreach, to increase its visibility and attract more backlinks.

Remember that DA is just one of many factors search engines consider when ranking websites. Focus on providing value to your audience and improving your website's overall quality, and your DA should naturally increase over time. Also, keep in mind that DA is specific to Moz, and other SEO tools may use different metrics to measure a website's authority.

Questions:

1. Illustrate about Article Writing and Submission
2. Sketch out feed Do's and Don't' s of Link Building
3. Compare social bookmarking and social Networking.
4. How to build blog posting and how to develop comment Writing
5. Illustrate how domain authority is used and how to increase that.
6. In what case Article Writing and submission is used.
7. Define Search Engine Submissions.
8. Explain about Directory Submission.
9. Summarize about Blog Posting and Comment Writing.
10. Classify about Domain Authority& How to Increase